DESIGN
GROW
SELL

Get the eBook of

DESIGN GROW SELL

for free

As a buyer of the printed version of this book you can download the **eBook version** free of charge in formats compatible with Kindle, iPad, Kobo and other eBook readers. Just point your camera or tablet phone at the code above or go to:

ebooks.harriman-house.com/designgrowsell

DESIGN
GROW
SELL

A GUIDE TO STARTING AND RUNNING A SUCCESSFUL *gardening business* FROM YOUR HOME

by Sophie Davies

A Brightword book | www.brightwordpublishing.com

HARRIMAN HOUSE LTD
3A Penns Road
Petersfield
Hampshire
GU32 2EW
GREAT BRITAIN

Tel: +44 (0)1730 233870 | Fax: +44 (0)1730 233880
Email: enquiries@harriman-house.com | Website: www.harriman-house.com

Copyright © 2013 Harriman House Ltd. Images © iStockphoto.com.
First published in Great Britain in 2013

Country Living is a registered trade mark of The National Magazine Company Limited

The right of Sophie Davies to be identified as the Author has been asserted in accordance with the Copyright, Design and Patents Act 1988.

ISBN: 9781908003393

British Library Cataloguing in Publication Data | A CIP catalogue record for this book can be obtained from the British Library.

Book printed and bound in the UK
Set in Caslon and joeHand 2

Contents

Preface

Who this book is for

This book is aimed at people who love plants and gardening and want to find a way of turning their gardening hobby into a business.

It is for those dreaming of a second or third career who, frustrated by their existing jobs, want to get outdoors and be creative. It is for green-fingered homemakers who, after a career break to raise their children, want to work flexible hours. It is for those with stressful office jobs who want to leave the big smoke for a life in the country.

And it is for those just starting out on their career, who want to do the thing they love first time round.

What this book does

The aim of the next 180 pages is not to be a substitute for getting the right training, nor is it intended to be a definitive guide. But I hope it will give you a starting point, an overview of what life running your own gardening business is like, with honest and first-hand experience from those in the know.

The next ten chapters will look at:

1. coming up with your initial idea and developing it
2. inspiring individuals with bold garden businesses
3. choosing a course and getting trained
4. the technicalities of company set-up
5. the practicalities of company set-up
6. getting started and building a customer base
7. building a network of contacts
8. promoting your business
9. dealing with customers
10. growing your gardening business.

And finally, some words of wisdom to send you on the way from those successful gardening businessmen and women profiled in this book.

With thanks to

With many thanks to all those interviewed, who gave up their time to answer so many questions. They are:

Case studies

Alan Shipp, The National Collection of Hyacinths

Alison Marsden, Gardening by Design

Angus White, Architectural Plants

Caroline De Lane Lea and Louise Cummins, Gardenmakers

Caroline Knight, The Quiet Gardener

Georgia Miles, The Sussex Flower School

Gill Chamberlain, Garden Rescue

Gilly Pollock, British Plant Nursery Guide

Graham Gough, Marchants Hardy Plants

Guy Watts and James Gubb, Streetscape

Hugo Bugg Landscapes

James Alexander-Sinclair Garden and Landscape Design

Jimi Blake, Hunting Brook Gardens

Juiet Sargeant Garden Design

Lisa Rawley, Fleur de Lys

Louise Dowding Garden Design

Mark Yabsley, Pod Garden Design

Mike Kitchen, Rocket Gardens

Sam Ellson, The Traditional Flower Company

Sarah Mead, Yeo Valley's Organic Garden

Sean Walter, The Plant Specialist

Sue Gray, Damhead Nursery

Experts

Denise Cadwallader, Garden Arts garden design and Capel Manor College lecturer

Gary Edwards, gardener and founder of The Gardeners Guild

Hannah Powell, communications consultant for Perrywood garden centre and nursery

Jonnie Wake, landscape contractor turned designer, Landmark Gardens, and The English Gardening School lecturer

Moira Farnham, garden designer and co-founder of the Garden Design School

Paul Cooling, chairman of Coolings Nurseries

Plus the team at *Country Living*

Ruth Chandler, features editor

Stephanie Donaldson, gardening editor

Rachel Taylor, intern

And other *Country Living* contributors to this book

Catherine Butler

Charlie Ryrie

Hester Lacey

Paula McWaters

Introduction

Have you ever gazed out of your office window on a sunny day and thought how much better it would be to be outdoors, or flicked through the pages of your favourite gardening magazine with longing? Maybe you have pictured yourself, secateurs in hand, running a high-end garden-maintenance business, or dreamed of a studio space in your attic with a drawing board on which you can produce garden plans…

The next ten chapters will look at the diverse business opportunities that exist just outside your back door (and the back doors of others). We'll look at being a commercial gardener, a garden or interior landscape designer, running your own independent nursery, opening your garden to the public, becoming a gardening coach or speaker, even opening your own gardening school.

We'll trace the process of starting a business – from developing your initial idea, taking advantage of training and internship opportunities, right the way through to company set-up. We'll cover ideas for how to get your first job, how to promote yourself and finally, when you are ready, how to expand your skills and grow your business.

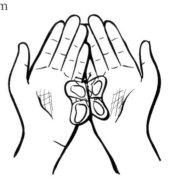

Ten years ago, seduced by TV gardening makeover shows and glossy coffee table gardening books, I gave up writing magazine articles to become a garden design student. I wish I had appreciated the importance of a sound horticultural grounding back then, and understood that gardens take time to get established and mature. I wish I had determined a niche for myself before starting out, and formulated a solid business plan. And if only I had grasped the value of networking and known what forms of advertising would and wouldn't work (to save on some costly and ultimately pointless expenditure). More importantly, it would have been great to have known how much support and advice could be gained from business start-up organisations and joining the appropriate trade body from the start.

I very much hope this book will answer the kinds of questions I had back then and provide exactly the sort of advice and inspiration that I needed.

The following chapters catalogue the experiences of 22 inspiring individuals who each give a frank account of what setting up and running your own gardening business is really like and what they have learned. There are top business tips from them, as well as others who are experts in their fields, plus contact details of useful websites, publications, individuals, organisations and charities that may be of interest or able to help.

Good luck with your exciting new venture. I hope it proves to be a happy and fulfilling one.

Sophie Davies

CHAPTER 1

Coming up with Your Initial Idea

D o you dream of opening a nursery like Graham Gough of Marchants Hardy Plants in Chapter 6, or of running a busy practice like designers Gardenmakers in Chapter 5? Are you a keen grower with a green business plan like Mike Kitchen of Rocket Gardens in Chapter 10? Have you spotted a niche like Garden Rescue's Gill Chamberlain in Chapter 7?

WHAT DO YOU WANT TO DO?

The first step in setting up a successful gardening business is knowing what you want to do. Here are some of the options out there:

Garden maintenance

You could offer basic gardening-round services, such as lawn-cutting, hedge-trimming, weeding and leaf clearance, or a high-end garden manicure service. You could develop expertise and offer a specialist pruning or planting service, ultimately overseeing the development of large country gardens or small estates. You could recruit a team and offer fence repairs, pond maintenance, or installation of irrigation systems as specialist or add-on services. Whichever, you will need plenty of energy and sound plant knowledge.

Garden design

Garden design requires a great many different skills, both creative and organisational, plus an understanding of how things are built. As a fully-fledged designer, you would produce outline garden master plans and planting plans for clients, as well as detailed construction drawings. You could also be asked to undertake simple site surveys, project monitor building works and supply and plant the plants. Some designers specialise in, for example, contemporary, historical or coastal gardens, or offer maintenance or even garden building as part of their service.

Or you could decide potted plants and troughs are more your thing and specialise in roof terraces and balconies, or become an interior landscape designer, brightening up shops, terraces and homes with your beautiful planted displays.

Independent nursery

Independent nursery owners tend to have a passion for a particular planting style or type of plant such as exotics, ferns or grasses, and this often forms the basis of their enterprise.

What plants you sell will depend on your interests, your expertise and to some extent your location. You may start out in a small way, opening your garden or field to the public and selling a few of your seasonal favourites. Or you could rent or buy some land and invest in greenhouses and polytunnels to grow on a bigger scale and sell through farmers markets and plant fairs, perhaps also opening a retail outlet of your own.

Open garden

You may decide to open your garden to the public (should you be lucky enough to have one large and beautiful enough to do so), run garden-related courses and events there, perhaps sell plants and even open up a teashop, as Sarah Mead later in this chapter has done. You could do a trial run and open your garden a few days a year under the National Gardens Scheme, raising money for charity as you do so.

Teaching horticulture

You could offer a garden-coaching service in peoples' gardens, showing them how to grow vegetables, prune trees, reshape their lawn and make the most of their outdoor spaces. You could develop specialist knowledge and give talks or lectures. You could even open your own school like Georgia Miles' The Sussex Flower School in Chapter 8.

Your gardening business may combine two or more of the above, as many of those profiled in this book do. There are nurseries that run workshops or offer maintenance, designers who appear on TV or open their gardens to the public, and gardeners who coach.

Or you could become a garden writer, submitting articles to magazines and newspapers; a garden historian, helping owners of grand gardens restore them to their former glory. You might even organise garden tours.

The next chapter looks at some more unusual ideas for gardening businesses – don't be afraid to think outside the box!

FURTHER RESEARCH

Finding your niche

The question is, do you *really* want to go head-to-head with the big players, or will finding a niche form the basis of your business? Perhaps you have spotted a gap in the market for a front garden design service, an independent nursery in your area or some expert topiary.

Garden designer and lecturer Denise Cadwallader says:

"There are designers who do just contemporary gardens. There are others that grow vegetables and help people become greener with less hard landscaping and water-saving devices. But don't overspecialise to the point that you have no market."

The competition

Once you have determined your niche, research the competition. Whose are those logoed vans that you see outside the best-kept gardens? What services does – and doesn't – that company offer? Where is the business based? What areas does it cover? And what does it charge?

Do your homework and check out competitors' websites. Who are your customers going to be and are there enough of them to keep you going? Is there really space for another such gardening business in your area or will you have to come up with a new angle or travel further afield for work? Will your nursery need to offer a mail order and online service in addition to local sales?

What a business involves

You need to know what your chosen enterprise entails. What's it like, day to day, running your own plant nursery or project monitoring a team of garden builders on a muddy construction site? Can you issue instructions? Are you tough enough to run your own show? Do you mind the cold and the rain?

Speak to people who are already working in your chosen field. Get in touch with a local garden designer and offer to help out on planting jobs, volunteer as a gardener for the National Trust or get a job at a local plant nursery and see how it's done.

Coolings Nurseries chairman Paul Cooling says:

> "Before you start out, I think you need some experience of running a business. People think: 'Wouldn't it be lovely to do this in my garden?' But they don't really understand the scale of things or, for example, the basics of VAT."

FINANCE

What it costs

Starting a new career is a big financial commitment – there's the cost of studying, of buying equipment and then of setting yourself up. Many of the people profiled in this book agree the first three years are especially tough. How will you manage? Perhaps you have an understanding partner who is happy to support you through this time. Perhaps you have money put by to keep you going for a while. Perhaps you could ease the transition by continuing to work part-time, if you have the time and energy to do so.

Well-established garden designer Denise Cadwallader started out offering a garden maintenance service which she kept up for the first three years while building up her design work. She was offered a teaching post at Capel Manor College and this gave her the financial freedom to reduce her maintenance work and increase the design-side of her earnings.

What you make

What can you expect to get paid? (And will this be enough to live on, once business running costs have been taken away?) Garden designers I spoke to while researching this book were reluctant to reveal their earnings, though £30 to £60 an hour for design work seems to be typical (starting lower in the early days when producing plans takes longer, and then increasing). However, operating costs and the time spent actually running your own business and managing your accounts cannot be charged to the client. One well-established, part-time garden designer I spoke to revealed they had earned £20,000 the previous year.

The Gardeners Guild organisation states that a domestic gardener should aim to earn a minimum of £100 to £150 a day, according to their level of expertise and location, though again the cost of equipment, insurance and accountant's fees comes out of this. Garden coaching pays around £25–£30 an hour (and your time is chargeable not only while you are at the clients' garden, but also when back in your office writing up their report). Garden writing pays in the region of £300 per 1,000-

word feature and Garden Media Guild members charge anything between £40 and £400 (plus travel expenses) for public speaking, depending on the speaker's profile and location.

How much money you make from running your own nursery or opening your garden to the public is down to the scale of your operation, the number of customers you attract and how enterprising you are. It depends what you want. For some it's a paid hobby, and as long as charging people to come and look round their garden or buy a few plants from their nursery generates enough income to cover its upkeep or provide a small additional income, that's enough. For others, it needs to be a more commercial concern, in which case diversification is a must.

The importance of passion

While researching this book *passion* was the word that came up over and over again. Everyone interviewed – from a bulb expert to head gardener, nursery owner to gardening personality – enthused about their job.

Running your own gardening business might not make you a million, but it does mean spending much of your working life outdoors and doing something that you love. It means the luxury of choosing your hours (though be prepared for hard work, especially in the peak growing season) and enormous job satisfaction.

Garden designer, columnist and TV presenter James Alexander-Sinclair sums it up:

> "Rather than doing it for the money, I do it because I have an urge to leave the bits of the world upon which I am let loose a little more beautiful than they were before I arrived."

CASE STUDY
ANGUS WHITE
ARCHITECTURAL PLANTS

I will never forget my first trip to Architectural Plants. With bamboo forests rustling in the wind, row upon row of the tallest palm trees I had ever seen and a rather smart, colonial-style wooden hut housing the company HQ, it was as if a piece of the tropics had been scooped up and dropped down in the middle of the English countryside.

The story of its founder Angus White is likewise unconventional. Annoyed he couldn't buy the exotic, sculptural and evergreen plants he wanted, Angus decided, quite simply, to grow and sell them himself from a sloping, three-acre donkey field he owned in West Sussex. He called his new nursery Architectural Plants.

A furniture designer rather than a horticulturalist by trade, he made regular trips to Wakehurst Place in West Sussex (*www.kew.org/visit-wakehurst*) – a vast 465-acre estate with a walled garden and woodlands, home to Kew's Millennium Seed Bank – to learn more about trees, scribbling down lists of his favourites.

"People who run nurseries usually have letters after their names," he says. "I was just full of beans and dead keen."

He recalls tracking down ten *Nothofagus dombeyi* (Dombey's Southern Beech) at RHS Garden Wisley (*www.rhs.org.uk*), buying eight to propagate from and thoughtfully leaving the last two for some other like-minded shopper. He returned some months later and found them still there.

"That should have told me there was no existing market for the kind of plants I wanted to grow, but I was driven. I wasn't so much looking for a gap in the market as doing something I wanted to and nothing was going to stop me. It was a kind of madness!"

He conducted some market research in the form of focus groups. The results proved at worst depressing and at best inconclusive, but Angus went ahead anyway.

With the help of an accountant friend, who was a farmer and grower by background, Angus developed "a bit of a business plan" establishing the basics such as "projected sales and working out a price per plant according to pot size. All the standard stuff and, like most business plans, it proved to be utter nonsense in the end, but sounded good at the time." He recruited Kew Gardens propagator Peter Tindley to help and he is still there, 20 years on.

Ordering a vast, 44 × 100 foot greenhouse signalled the point of no return. Then there were trenches to dig, power, drainage and a state-of-the-art fogging system to install (which allows tricky, tender exotics to root without rotting in the ground). "Then there was irrigation to learn about, fertiliser, different types of compost. In the early days, the task just seemed overwhelming," Angus says.

But by 1990, Architectural Plants was ready to open its doors to a largely unenlightened public. A half-page article by the esteemed garden writer Anna Pavord in *The Independent* about this bold new nursery in Horsham put it on the map.

Ten years after opening, the market for exotic plants had become well catered for, and cut-priced competition from the big nursery chains kicked in. Architectural Plants responded by diversifying into garden design and construction, and offering a planting and creative maintenance service. "Trying harder," Angus says.

Today, with a Queens Award under its belt (for Enterprise in Innovation and the only horticultural business to have one), Architectural Plants has expanded, with two garden designers on the team plus between two and five gardeners at any one time. A brand new, 35-acre site is due to open at the end of 2012 on land leased from nearby Chichester College's agricultural Brinsbury Campus as a result of private investment. The new nursery will replace the original site at Horsham and a second which opened just outside Chichester.

Angus now has a co-director but has retained control of the company and remains resolutely hands on. He has started an on-the-spot design service for clients, turning up with a lorry load of plants, placing as appropriate, planting and then taking the rest away – one of the advantages of having your own nursery.

> "The idea behind Architectural Plants is still very much the same as it was 20 years ago. I think my advice to anyone setting out is stick to your guns and be very, very cautious about listening to other people."

★ *www.architecturalplants.com*

CASE STUDY
SARAH MEAD
YEO VALLEY'S ORGANIC GARDEN

There was a time when it didn't seem to matter how scruffy an organic garden appeared – it was the techniques that were paramount and making it look nice was, at best, a secondary consideration.

This was understandable in the pioneering days when there was a great deal of trial and error involved, biological pest controls were non-existent and organic potting composts had to be home produced. Now it is pretty much impossible to tell a good organic plot from one that is conventionally cultivated. A shining example of this is Yeo Valley's Organic Garden at Holt Farm in Somerset, where underlying environmental credentials are swathed in a cloak of beauty.

Skilful design and inspired planting have transformed six-and-a-half acres of farmland into a sophisticated country garden that is the only organic ornamental garden to be certified by the Soil Association.

Holt Farm is home to Tim and Sarah Mead, who run their organic family dairy business on the surrounding land. Twenty years ago when Sarah arrived at the farm, the garden consisted of a rockery and some roses. She had grown up in London and had "no interest in gardening whatsoever". But, learning as she went, she opened the evolving garden in aid of the National Gardens Scheme four years later.

Sarah admits she made mistakes along the way and, as the garden gradually expanded, realised she was in need of some expert assistance and guidance. The team of three gardeners she has gathered around her is a happy and harmonious crew. They have enabled her to create a garden that is inspirational and showcases the very best in organic techniques. "We are committed to trying to prove that organic doesn't have to mean recycled tyres and plastic bottles," she says.

Although this was the case from the outset, Sarah became increasingly fed up with overhearing visitors to her garden say: "I wonder how organic they really are?" So, in 2008, she took the bold decision to close the garden to visitors for two years and apply for certification from the Soil Association. This rigorous, ongoing process brings the garden in line with the surrounding farm and confirms to visitors that it is run in accordance with the strictest organic standards.

There have been considerable challenges to overcome, particularly a serious infestation of bindweed in the gravel garden that necessitated emptying it of all its plants, followed by the entire team excavating to a depth of two metres with the help of a mini digger and removing three whole trailer loads of bindweed roots. It took a month and, though it was a task none of them would wish to repeat, it did provide the opportunity for the area to be redesigned and replanted – a silver lining of sorts.

While growers of organic vegetables are wonderfully served these days with numerous suppliers of seeds and young plants, things aren't quite so straightforward for those wishing to create an organic ornamental garden. So Sarah has invested in a greenhouse where she and her team now grow most of their own from seeds and cuttings. Further, the garden is managed on a closed system which means the potting composts, liquid feeds, soil improvers and compost tea used there are made on site with materials from the plot itself.

The garden opens from April to September and last year attracted 5,000 visitors, mainly from the UK. Sarah and her team give tours personally. This means that during the busy periods there is simply not enough gardening time to carry out major works, so the garden closes over winter for essential maintenance, to undertake new projects and to plant 25,000 bulbs for the following year.

"There was never an end plan, just blind passion for a newly acquired addiction," Sarah says. The next step is to make the garden more commercial and visitor-friendly. To this end, a proper tea room, public toilets and car park have been built. There is a summer open air theatre and fundraising lectures and workshops by such gardening personalities as Sarah Raven, Bunny Guinness and Toby Buckland.

"My advice to anyone thinking of opening their garden to the public is to make sure you like people. It sounds obvious I know, but you would be amazed how many people patently prefer their plants," Sarah says.

★ *www.theorganicgardens.co.uk*

{ CHAPTER 2 }

Thinking Outside the Box

Running your own gardening business doesn't necessarily mean setting up a straightforward maintenance company, opening up a nursery, becoming a landscape designer or a gardening coach as those profiled in this chapter show.

The inspiring gardeners we will meet here have used their love of plants and gardening to carve out exciting, unusual businesses doing something they love.

ETHICAL BUSINESSES

Streetscape (profiled below) is one of a growing number of social enterprises, thriving despite an economic downturn. These companies exist to bring about positive social and/or environmental change, investing money made back into the business, rather than paying out large salaries to its owners, or dividends to shareholders (as it has none). You can find out more at *www.socialenterprise.org.uk*.

London-based Roots and Shoots (*www.rootsandshoots.org.uk*) is an early example, set up in 1982 by trained horticulturist Linda Phillips who has since received an MBE for her services to young people. Her enterprise has helped those with difficulties at school prepare for the world of work, with English, Maths, ICT, retail and gardening skills.

My local social enterprise, Tuppenny Barn Organic Project (*www.tuppennybarn.com*), where I go each Thursday to collect the delicious homegrown organic vegetables it sells, is putting the finishing touches to an eco-friendly education centre, where schoolchildren can come and learn about sustainable practices and how food is grown.

CASE STUDY

Guy Watts and James Gubb
Streetscape

It's Monday morning in south-east London and four young men are sitting in a makeshift classroom. They are apprentices on Streetscape's one-year City & Guilds Level 2 Diploma in Work-Based Horticulture and today they are learning how to lay sub-base before going out on site to put the theory into practice.

Founders Guy Watts and James Gubb set up Streetscape in 2010 to provide on-the-job training for long-term unemployed 18–25 year-olds, giving them the chance of a career in horticulture. Under the watchful eye of head landscape gardener Luke Conrad, they undertake real-life design, landscaping and maintenance projects in and around the city.

Guy has gardened since childhood. His role is to attract sponsors, win business and raise funds to pay for the training. He is also Streetscape's second landscaper, focused on soft landscaping and garden maintenance. James' task is to manage Streetscape's operations and develop corporate relationships which offer financial support and advice.

Their enterprise has two community partners – Stepney City Farm and Myatts Fields Park – the latter where the organisation is based, its apprentices are trained and young, would-be horticulturalists can go on taster days.

Last year Streetscape took on its first two future gardeners – who have since gone on to get landscaping jobs – and this year has taken on four more.

"When we started out, we had a lot of blank dates on the calendar and work came through family or friends," says James. "We had a couple of articles in local papers and that helped. We delivered fliers, we knocked on doors."

By February of the following year, Streetscape was booked up two months ahead. Now it has enough work to sustain two teams and is getting word-of-mouth referrals.

Quite an achievement in itself, but what makes it all the more impressive is that while James worked as a full-time Streetscape project manager for the first two years, Guy worked only part-time on the venture, in the evenings and weekends, while holding down a full-time job which he has since given up. As a social enterprise, Streetscape's sponsorship and funding pays modest apprentice salaries, while it is only the money generated through jobs that pays Guy, James and Luke.

The company has completed around 40 to 50 client gardens to-date. On-the-job training means the work still has to be up to scratch. To make sure it is, Guy and James allow a little extra time to get jobs done so that any mistakes can be rectified as they go along. The fact that Streetscape's Checkatrade score average stands at 9.6/10 is testament to this professional mindset.

> "Part of our sales pitch is that our work is of a high standard, but also that it helps get young people into work. If it takes a couple of extra days, no one seems to mind," says James. "I love the mix of being outside, helping on site, seeing the progression of the apprentices and solving all those little problems. First, it was how do we get this business started? Then it was how do we get our apprentices jobs? Now it is how can we make it better next year?"

Guy's top tip for running your own successful gardening business is: "Find a partner you believe in and trust 100% and whose skills compliment yours. I think I have the perfect business partner in James."

★ *www.streetscape.org.uk*

Open gardens

Plant hunter Jimi Blake's garden outside Dublin (profiled below) is one of a handful of privately-owned gems that open to the public – a place where expert plantspeople can showcase their outstanding gardening skills. Another such is East Ruston Old Vicarage in Norfolk (*www.e-ruston-oldvicaragegardens.co.uk*). Here owners Alan Gray and Graham Robeson have created a series of spectacular garden rooms across a 32-acre site surrounding their home.

Turning your garden into a business that generates enough money not only to cover its maintenance but to work commercially and pay a wage, requires not just charging an entrance fee but some clever creative thinking. It's about providing add-ons such as plant sales, holding lectures and talks, writing articles, perhaps even a book about your garden, having a tearoom selling organic lunches and afternoon tea. Sarah Mead of Yeo Valley's Organic Garden confirms:

> "If you want to stand a chance of making any money, then a tearoom is a must."

CASE STUDY
JIMI BLAKE
HUNTING BROOK GARDENS

Hunting Brook Gardens is set in undulating countryside an hour's drive from Dublin and opens to the public on various weekends throughout the year, from spring until autumn and by appointment throughout. Owner Jimi Blake's planting style is exotic, naturalistic and experimental and has visitors reaching for pens and paper to take notes. He also runs courses here, sells plants, gives tours to the busloads of tourists that arrive in spring and summer, as well as lecturing in between times and selling seeds and plants.

Jimi trained in horticulture at The National Botanic Gardens in Glasnevin, Dublin (*www.botanicgardens.ie*) and then gardened for 12 years at Airfield (*www.airfield.ie*), one of the city's public gardens, overseeing its major restoration as head gardener. When the chance came to create his own 20-acre plot in Wicklow on his parents' farming estate, he didn't hesitate.

Building a wooden house for himself and a polytunnel for his plants, he initially held courses in the house's kitchen; these have since moved to the purpose-built garden room, while Jimi's own kitchen now houses the tearoom.

Jimi quit his job at Airfield in September 2001 and opened his garden the following spring. The first visitors, many of whom still return each year, saw the garden in its very early stages. "It was very low-key to start with. I was working with what I had as I didn't want to spend a fortune," Jimi says.

He operates more or less as a one-man band, running the business and course programme, as well as undertaking most of the maintenance himself, with the help of volunteers on Fridays throughout the summer. It's a fair exchange – Jimi trades an hour's tutoring for half a day's graft in the garden. "I have to keep checking with myself that I am doing what I love and change things if I'm not," he says.

And he has adjusted his business in response to the recession. Luxury cookery courses, for example, are no longer in such demand. His practical One Year Plants Persons Course, on the other hand, is double-booked, while at 2pm on garden open days, paid-up visitors are invited to a free class given by Jimi. These, too, are busy.

"My advice to anyone looking to start their own gardening business would be, don't put blinkers on. You need to do lots of different things to generate an income," Jimi says. "Every person who comes through the gate, I think 'How can I increase what they spend?'"

For example, add to the €6 entrance fee an extra €7 spent on plants, and a further €12 spent in the tearoom – and your grand total is €25.

In addition to open days, courses, lecturing and garden tours, Jimi also rents out 60 allotments on the site from February to December each year and hires out the garden room for corporate functions and holistic events. You can even get married in the gardens or the woods.

Jimi makes sure he gets an email address from "pretty much everyone who comes through the gate" and sends them a monthly newsletter. He does some magazine advertising and promotes his garden through Facebook. He invited well-known gardeners such as Carol Klein to come and give talks at Hunting Brook in the early days. This built the garden's reputation through word of mouth which, in turn, led to press coverage.

"The key is to try to do something a bit different. There are lots of lovely gardens with run-of the-mill herbaceous borders. The question is how to stand out?"

★ *www.huntingbrook.com*

SPECIALIST BUSINESSES

Conservatory plant expert Lisa Rawley (profiled below) has created a thriving business using her super-specialist horticultural skills, much like hyacinth expert Alan Shipp in Chapter 5. Becoming a specialist, with a market (pretty much) all of your own, can be a good way to secure a loyal customer base. Gardener Jake Hobson of Niwaki (*www.niwaki.com*), for example, specialises in Japanese pruning techniques, sells the tools to do it and writes books on the subject. I once met and interviewed a man who had carved out a niche and made his living from clipping shapes in clients' gardens out of overgrown box.

Then there are nurseries such as Long Acre Plants in Somerset that sell plants by mail order for a particular situation – in this case plants for woodland and shade (*www.plantsforshade.co.uk*).

More generally, you can make a name for having a preferred plant palette or a particular, distinctive style. Ten years ago I worked for a very good garden designer called Lynne Marcus (*www.lynnemarcus.com*) who has an upscale landscape design company in London with a definite contemporary look – with clear geometry, crisp York stone paving, prolific borders and smart green lawns. I came across one of her gardens featured in *Gardens Illustrated* recently and could tell, before I even looked at the captions, that it was one of hers.

CASE STUDY
LISA RAWLEY
FLEUR DE LYS

Lisa Rawley is an interior landscape designer who grows, designs and installs planting schemes for grand-scale conservatories, greenhouses and orangeries. In fact her business is so super-niched that she is in the unusual position of having no direct competition at all, but travels for work instead, from her base just outside Fittleworth in West Sussex, across the south coast to Wales, up into Gloucestershire, over to London and east into Suffolk. She undertakes around six new projects each year, as well as maintenance of existing schemes, and grows about a third of her own plants from a 56 × 21 foot greenhouse at her nursery – a short walk from home.

Much of Lisa's work comes through word-of-mouth referral from satisfied clients. RHS Chelsea Flower Show, where her company Fleur de Lys takes an annual stand (and won a gold medal in 2010), is another valuable source of new work. As is the internet. "I am astonished how this has taken off," she says.

Creating an ornamental display of plants not normally seen side by side and that looks wonderful all year round is a very particular process and Lisa charges a fee for going to see the client and writing an in-depth proposal for a scheme, detailing sizes, pots and plants. "People often know what they want. At least the look, though they don't know names," she says.

In contrast to exterior landscape designers, perhaps because they are up against such stiff competition, Lisa is generous in sharing ideas with her would-be clients. Putting them in touch with other businesses, with Lisa's network of greenhouse companies, blind manufacturers, furniture makers, heating and ventilation companies often clinches the deal.

Once schemes are complete, Lisa gives care instructions to the client and/or their gardener as well as offering a twice-yearly maintenance service. And so, between mid-March and mid-June and then again in the autumn, Lisa takes to the road, revisiting past projects for re-potting, pruning, training, tidying, redesigning spaces, feeding, pest control and adding new species.

Lisa's interest in plants started as a child. She grew up in Essex with parents who were keen gardeners and their garden was "enormous". She studied horticulture at Writtle College (*www.writtle.ac.uk*) and spent her second year there on a fruit farm in Sussex, loved it and returned to the farm when she qualified, later becoming a strawberry consultant with the Farm Advisory Services Team (*www.fastltd.co.uk*). But keen to be her own boss and to get back to hands-on cultivation, Lisa started looking for a business opportunity.

"I noticed there were a lot of conservatories being built and I knew I had the skills to grow plants for them."

Some early publicity in the business section of *The Times* meant Lisa's new company got off to a flying start. This meant setting up the company without a business loan and, within two years, she was supporting herself.

Despite opportunities, Lisa has resisted taking on staff, a site or pushing into retail sales.

"I have never done it, partly out of fear of borrowing money. Plus the bigger the business got, the more agitated I would become. And it would take me away from what I really enjoy. I would be managing staff rather than fiddling with plants."

This means Lisa works principally on her own, collaborating from time to time with gardener Louise Elliot who lives nearby. While the conservatory side is business as usual, Lisa and Louise are also working on upgrading the gardens at nearby historical Bignor Park (*www.bignorpark.co.uk*).

"It is full time. If you're not actually designing, you are buying plants or looking after the nursery, growing the plants, dealing with pest control. It's a lot of work but I love it."

Lisa's top tip is this:

"Always ask yourself if you have done the best possible job for a client. If the answer is *no*, then you need to think carefully about what it is people are asking you for and how well you are meeting their needs."

★ *www.conservatoryplants.co.uk*

THE CAREER CHANGER

The Traditional Flower Company founder Sam Ellson's former life was as a highly-paid fashion merchandising director but she gave this up to work on the family farm growing flowers. She is typical of a number of others profiled in this book, among them doctor-turned-garden-designer Juliet Sargeant, landscape-architect-turned-nursery-owner Sue

Gray and software-manager-turned-garden-coach Alison Marsden who have changed their careers to pursue a dream. Suzy Greaves (*www.suzygreaves.com*), a writer, life coach and much-quoted expert on this subject, says:

> "We are realising that fulfilment is not based on how much money you earn or what car you drive. A portfolio career is becoming the norm – where we create businesses at the kitchen table and can pick the kids up from school if we so wish."

Self-employment brings flexibility and freedom but also uncertainty. Many therefore spread the risk with different income streams.

> "Many of my clients have an internet shop selling their homemade products and work freelance for a couple of clients, as well as having a stand at seasonal fairs selling their wares. It is hard work but ultimately you are creating a life you love," she says.

CASE STUDY
SAM ELLSON
THE TRADITIONAL FLOWER COMPANY

Sam Ellson's journey to work could not be much more different to five years ago. She slips out of her farmhouse door, secateurs in hand, passing through an old gate that separates her garden from the 100 acres of farmland worked by her husband Robin. After 20 years of working for high street fashion brands and enduring a daily 130-mile commute

to Liverpool, Sam finally swapped her briefcase for a wooden trug and her office for a field of roses.

"I didn't have green fingers, just a vision," says Sam who, aside from a lifelong love of flowers, had no horticultural training at all before launching her cut-flower business, The Traditional Flower Company, which was featured in the June 2012 issue of *Country Living* Magazine. "I hadn't planted anything until ten years ago when I planted 200 roses in my garden. I was amazed by how they took off," she says.

Despite always yearning to run her own business, it was only when Sam was made redundant from her position as merchandising director of Littlewoods in 2005 that she began plotting her new direction. Rather than launching into her new venture blindly, she set about planning her now-thriving concern. "I wanted to do something on the farm but couldn't take away too much acreage from the sheep. Cut flowers were the perfect solution because you can do a lot in a small space." Her business now employs a team of three local girls and has a vintage country style that's attracted such a following it has weddings booked three years ahead.

Using her redundancy package as a buffer, Sam took a year out to test the viability of her idea and planted 4,000 rose bushes in an empty paddock. Five months later in mid-June 2007 they were in full bloom and picked, arranged into rustic bouquets, loaded onto her new retro-fitted van and bound for local farmers markets where she could experiment with prices and arrangements. "It showed me that what I was going to do involved hard graft but that I was going to love it," she says.

By the end of the year Sam was determined to make the business work but realised that to earn a full wage she had to think big. "I needed a polytunnel to extend my growing season and an extra 4,000 roses, 5,000 herbs and other foliage," she says. But without the capital to invest immediately, she let the business fall dormant while she returned to her old career, this time at Matalan, where after two years she had pulled together a six-figure sum.

Seven years on and The Traditional Flower Company has grown from a single planted paddock to four fields of six acres. A pig barn on the farm has been converted into a workshop. Sam also runs flower design workshops from a purpose-built shed in her garden and has opened her own flower shop in the nearby village. Her arrangements have won prestigious awards: a silver medal at RHS Hampton Court Palace Flower Show in 2010 and a Silver Gilt at RHS Flower Show Tatton Park the following year. And Sam has finally started to make a living from the company, with her and Robin now earning a 50/50 wage.

★ *www.traditionalflower.co.uk*

CHAPTER 3

Getting Qualified

So you've come up with an idea, looked at the competition and decided on your business. The next question is, are you an expert in your chosen area of gardening or do you need to go on a course to brush up on your skills?

You may be a great gardener but need to know about safe pesticide use. Perhaps you have developed amazing planting schemes for your own and friends' gardens but need to be taught how to present these to a client on paper. Maybe you have an idea for a fantastic new nursery but need to know how to run one.

How much training you need will depend not only on your gardening expertise and previous experience, but at what level you intend to operate. A fully-fledged garden designer creating garden master plans, the specification drawings to go with them and then project-monitoring a team of landscape contractors to get their gardens built, is going to need horticultural, design and drawing skills, as well as a sound understanding of how retaining walls, drainage and water features work.

Similarly, most people running their own nurseries will either have a previous career's growing experience behind them and/or have studied for RHS or other college certificates and gardened for many years.

It goes without saying that anyone running horticulture courses, offering a garden-coaching service or opening their garden to the public will need to know their subject. And, while there is no minimal training requirement to become a gardener, The Gardeners Guild demands at least one horticultural qualification such as an NPTC licence to become a member.

Qualifications

Widely-available qualifications include:

* apprenticeships

* work-based training, including Lantra Awards and City & Guilds awards, certificates and diplomas

* vocational qualifications such as BTECs and NVQs

* RHS Certificates

* other college-awarded certificates and diplomas, including HNC and HND

* one-year diplomas from largely London-based private colleges

* degree courses, including BSc Hons in Horticulture/BA Hons in Garden Design and MA courses in Garden History and Garden Design.

The cost of studying varies and you would need to speak to your chosen college for an up-to-date price. As a rough guide, a City & Guilds Award in the Safe Use of Pesticides course could cost £200, part-time college study for an RHS Certificate is likely to set you back around £600, while a three-year degree course is in the region of £8,000 a year. Go to *www.hotcourses.com* and speak to individual course providers to find out what funding or loans might be available.

One-year garden design diplomas at private colleges, meanwhile, cost upwards of around £5,000 while the Inchbald School of Design (*www.inchbald.co.uk*), which has turned out such notable designers as Luciano Giubbilei, Marcus Barnett and Philip Nixon, charges £21,420.

Training providers

Changing career and retraining is a huge financial commitment. And I should know.

Ten years ago, unmarried, aged 30 and with a sizeable mortgage, I signed up to a one-year diploma at The English Gardening School and was probably the least financially secure person on the course. Though the time spent in the classroom totalled just ten hours a week, completing the necessary coursework needed to pass took up almost all the remainder of my time.

In the evenings, during the school holidays and at weekends, I worked for a local landscape design practice and frantically wrote magazine articles to pay the bills. It was a very tough year and I'm afraid my coursework suffered. (You can read about the experiences of another garden design student, Caroline Knight, later in this chapter.)

The following websites offer advice as well as lists of universities, colleges and other training providers offering horticulture, garden design and other related courses:

★ City & Guilds awards certificates in, for example, Health & Safety and safe use of pesticides which can be studied through secondary education colleges as well as independent providers. Go to *www.cityandguilds.com* or *www.nptc.org.uk* for more information and to find out where courses are run.

★ *Grow* is administered by the Institute of Horticulture and was set up to inform people about careers in the industry and boasts a fantastic training website. Go to *www.growcareers.info* for a detailed list of career opportunities including what qualifications are necessary, and a list of 99 colleges where you can get them.

★ LANTRA is the UK's Sector Skills Council for land-based industries and provides advice on career paths and where to get trained. Lantra Awards runs a series of short courses with training partners up and down the country, covering the use of chainsaws, ride-on mowers, pesticides, hedge cutters, etc. *www.lantra.co.uk*.

* RHS Qualifications range from a Level 1 Certificate in Practical Horticulture up to a Master of Horticulture (with Level 2 and 3 Certificates in between). These are available through RHS-approved centres and distance learning colleges. For a full list of both, (plus details on RHS volunteering and internships), go to *www.rhs.org.uk*.

* The Society of Garden Designers has a very thorough training page on its website with a course checklist for would-be students. It also offers a business-mentoring service for its new design graduates who sign up for pre-registered membership, as well as a list of colleges offering garden design courses. Go to *www.sgd.org.uk*.

Experience

While books and courses are good at teaching the theory, there is no substitute for hands-on experience. The complaint that there are too many designers and not enough people with proper plant knowledge in the industry is heard over and over again.

The Women's Farm & Garden Association (*www.wfga.org.uk*) set up WRAGS, or the Women Returners to Amenity Gardening Scheme in 1993 to help women get practical training for a career in horticulture. It arranges 15 hours on-the-job training per week over a year in a carefully sourced garden, under the supervision of its owner or head gardener, as well as organising an annual seminar in London which looks at the opportunities for employment (including self-employment) in gardening. The Christine Ladley Fund offers financial support to members to help with their studies. Grants are awarded in July and members must submit an application to the fund trustees.

Opportunities for apprenticeships and traineeships (paid and unpaid) are available through the National Trust's NT Academy, The National Trust for Scotland, the RHS and

Professional Gardeners Guild (*www.pgg.org.uk*), as well as at Kew, Edinburgh, other Botanical Gardens (contact your nearest for up-to-date details) and The Eden Project (*www.edenproject.com*). An increasing number of colleges, including Askham Bryan (*www.askham-bryan.ac.uk*), Capel Manor (*www.capel.ac.uk*), Merrist Wood (*www.merristwood.ac.uk*) and Pershore Colleges (*www.warwickshire.ac.uk*), also offer horticultural apprenticeships.

The National Trust and the RHS have vacancies for unpaid volunteers in their gardens, as do charitable trust-owned gardens such as Great Dixter (*www.greatdixter.co.uk*) in East Sussex and West Dean Gardens (*www.westdean.org.uk*) in West Sussex. Here, gardens supervisor Sarah Wain and her hard-working, ten-strong team are backed by an army of 40 volunteers, many of whom help out in tandem with studying for their RHS Certificates. It looks good on your CV and you never know what useful connections you might make.

CASE STUDY
CAROLINE KNIGHT
THE QUIET GARDENER (GARDENER AND GARDEN DESIGN STUDENT)

For the last five years Caroline Knight has run her own maintenance company, The Quiet Gardener, on the Kent/Sussex/Surrey borders where she lives. She describes herself as "an accidental" gardener. That is to say, one without formal training.

Three years ago, she decided this had to change. If she was presenting herself as an expert to an ever-growing client list and in the gardening articles she wrote for local magazines and newspapers, she thought she should officially become one. So she enrolled on a part-time Garden Design degree course at Hadlow College in Tonbridge, Kent.

She has written a blog for *The Guardian*, charting the highs and lows of her studies (*www.guardian.co.uk/profile/caroline-knight*).

Her choice of Hadlow College was determined by four factors:

1. location (a 15-mile drive from her house)

2. cost (she was lucky enough to be eligible for funding to cover some of the fees, though this is no longer readily available)

3. the quality of training (the course ticked all boxes by combining practical plant knowledge with creative skills, plus surveying, professional studies, ecology and conservation)

4. the duration of the course (part-time, over four years, to leave space for family life and continued maintenance work, albeit on a reduced schedule).

With three years down, and one to go, she has learnt a great deal.

"I had no idea how little I actually knew before. I used to feel embarrassed by my lack of in-depth knowledge and on more than one occasion mumbled unintelligible fictitious Latin in answer to plant identification queries."

And she is by no means the only one to admit to having done so. I have heard this same confession from a surprising number of other contributors to this book.

Caroline's advice to anyone setting themselves up as a gardener is to label themselves according to their level of expertise. "If I was taking on a gardener I would expect them to know about plants and gardens. If, however, I wanted a garden labourer, my expectations would not be so great," she explains.

From secretary to secateurs

Caroline sees herself as typical of women of her age (she is 54) and upbringing; pigeon-holed into traditional office jobs because of gender, rather than ability or interest. She even recalls striking a bargain with her well-intentioned parents, who agreed to let her leave school aged 16 provided she went to secretarial college.

She duly went on to take an office job, which led to a marketing role and finally freelance writing. And then, when "the computer screen became too much of a permanent view", she began supplementing her work with garden maintenance.

It started with a friend whose garden had become overgrown and neglected. Caroline was charged with putting it right. "My favourite, favourite job is to go in and make something like that beautiful," she says, and she hasn't looked back.

The Quiet Gardener name and concept comes from Caroline's philosophy that developing your own gardening business should be a gentle, organic process that relies on growing your reputation as you work away quietly in people's gardens. The quality of the work, she believes, should speak for you. She has never advertised and is amazed at how much work comes her way.

Once her course is finished, Caroline plans to carry on as before "but with the benefit of greater wisdom", ideally expanding sideways into sustainable design. Her top tip to anyone embarking on career-changing study such as this is:

"A course like mine should not be undertaken lightly. It is not something that can be fitted in easily around a busy life. Studying part-time sounds quite relaxed but, when you are trying to keep many balls in the air, it is fraught and you need an understanding family who are prepared to be ignored for four years. There is absolutely no room or time for additional stresses and if something goes askew during my last year I will have to defer or abandon my studies."

CASE STUDY

JULIET SARGEANT
GARDEN DESIGNER AND LECTURER

Society of Garden Designers (SGD) vice chairperson Juliet Sargeant is a doctor-turned-Brighton-based garden designer whose gardens have been featured in *Coast* and *Gardenlife* magazines, as well as on Channel 4 and Meridian Television. She is co-author of planting book *New Naturalism* and also teaches at KLC School of Design (*www.klc.co.uk*) where she devised, and now runs, part-time courses in garden design.

Juliet started out on this career path 20 years ago and, coming from an academic background, doing a degree seemed to her to be the right thing to do. There were three garden design degree courses on offer at the time – at Writtle, Capel Manor and Hadlow Colleges – and she plumped for Capel Manor where, for the next four years (she took a year out to have a baby), she studied everything from garden design to photography and life drawing.

"I just loved the course. We really had time to immerse ourselves in the art of garden design," she says. "If you have the time and resources, I really recommend a degree because it gives a balanced view of garden design."

After qualifying, she started off quite slowly, gradually building a client base and reputation first in London and then, when she and her family moved, in Brighton. She continued the learning process, meanwhile, working her way towards full SGD membership. "It was a confidence issue. I felt it was important. Even after three years' study, there was so much still to learn," she says.

Today Juliet's practice specialises in what she describes as "one-off, weird situations". That is to say, rural and rather awkward locations, including coastal, sloping, listed and sensitive sites, as well as those battered by wind, erosion, and deer and rabbit grazing. Currently under construction are:

★ A one-acre garden in an Area of Outstanding Natural Beauty (land designated by the government to be of national value and therefore protected by law). This means consultation with English Nature, as well as the local and parish councils. To make matters more complicated, the site floods in the spring and dries out in the summer. The solution? "To use plants adapted to those conditions," says Juliet. She found these by observing similar sites nearby, consulting experts, researching and finally drawing on her own plant knowledge. "All the time liaising with my clients and asking them to understand and accept the experimental nature of the project," she says.

★ A one-and-a-half-acre garden, half of which is agricultural land – which means it must be planted with productive crops – and the other half purely ornamental. "But the two halves must marry together into a unified and pleasing composition," Juliet says.

This problem-solving is what interests her.

> "People ring up and say: 'Have you done this before?' And I say: 'No, but I have the skills to research it and solve it'."

Juliet describes herself as "an educator at heart", and has been instrumental in setting up the SGD's mentoring scheme along the lines of what she experienced as a newly-trained doctor. She believes newly-qualified garden designers are at a disadvantage. While landscape architects finish their courses and go into an established practice for a period of mentored experience before becoming fully qualified, "garden design graduates often find themselves in a back bedroom working alone". The aim of the scheme is to support new SGD graduate members in the early days of setting up and running their own businesses. Now in its second trial year, it boasts 30 recruits and involves bimonthly group meetings headed up by an experienced designer.

What is Juliet's advice to anyone starting out now?

> "I don't think it's a good idea to present yourself as someone who offers everything to everyone. I just don't think it does to be a jack of all trades. Be focused and you will offer a better service."

Similarly, while garden design colleges claim to cover all bases, each has their individual strengths, and Juliet recommends looking for a course that will develop your particular interests.

★ *www.julietdesigns.co.uk*

CHAPTER 4

Forming a Company (Technicalities)

S o with qualifications and work experience under your belt, let's look at the technicalities of setting up a company.

COMPANY SET-UP

Write a business plan

What is your basic idea? Where do you want to go? And what are the stepping stones to get there?

That's what writing a business plan helps you to determine. The best business plans are ones that can be revisited (and, in time, extended) throughout the life of a business.

You can find plenty of examples of solid business plans on the internet (including high street bank websites). Mark Yabsley, who we meet later in this chapter, is something of an expert on this. His former job was as a Barclays small business manager. His business plan for Pod Garden Design, which he has been kind enough to let us see, includes the following:

* company name, plus introduction and background, including personnel, office location and company values

* ownership, management and delegation of responsibilities

* short, medium and long-term business objectives

* what services the company offers and its fees

* equipment – what the company owns

* key suppliers of plants and materials

* key partners, including other designers and landscape contractors

* SWOT Analysis – a list of Strengths, Weaknesses, Opportunities and Threats

* company marketing strategy and areas to expand

* general short, medium and long-term goals

* training to undertake, and ongoing professional development

* financial projections and funding proposals

* cash flow forecast (money in and out of the business bank account).

Structure your company

What's the best company set-up for you? It will depend on your circumstances and it's best to get advice from your accountant at the outset, or read up at *www.gov.uk* or *www.hmrc.gov.uk* before you make a final decision. Emily Coltman ACA, chief accountant at online accounting service FreeAgent (*www.freeagent.com*), aimed at small businesses and freelancers, takes us on a brief tour of the options . . .

Sole trader

Will you be a *sole trader*, i.e. a self-employed gardener, designer or gardening coach? Many new businesses start out this way as it is simple to set up and run – you register your business with HMRC and file a self-assessment tax return each year. "However, as a sole trader, there is no difference between you and the business. Legally you are the business and so if the business is sued, so are you," Emily explains.

Partnership

You could work in a *partnership* with someone else. Having others to bounce ideas off is a huge plus, but you should get legal advice at the outset in case one of you decides to quit. Once again, there is no legal difference between partners and a partnership – so if the business is sued, the partners could lose their own assets.

"Partners are also 'jointly and severally liable' for the partnership's debts," says Emily. "That means if one partner absconds with the business's cash, the others will have to pay any business bills personally."

Like a sole trader, each partner must register with HMRC. The business must also be registered. Each partner must then file a self-assessment tax return each year, and a return must be filed for the partnership too.

Broadly speaking, sole traders and partners are all self-employed. They pay income tax and class 4 National Insurance on their share of the business profits, plus a flat rate of class 2 National Insurance.

Limited company

"A *limited company* is a very popular business structure because it is possible to pay less tax overall when you run your business through one," explains Emily. Plus, because a limited company is a separate legal entity from its directors and shareholders, it is the company, not you personally, that becomes liable for any debts incurred (unless you've given personal guarantees or been found guilty of wrongdoing). A limited company doesn't need more than one director, who can also be the only owner (shareholder) of that company.

The disadvantage of a limited company is that it is more time-consuming and expensive to set up and run. As well as registering and filing annual accounts and an annual return with Companies House (*www.companieshouse.gov.uk*), the company must also register with HMRC and file a company tax return each year. Corporation tax is due on company profits made and you need to speak to an accountant to establish the most tax-efficient way to take money out of the business.

VAT

VAT is a tax you must register for with HMRC and charge to your clients once your annual VAT-able sales go over a set limit (currently £77,000). You can register sooner if you wish and claim back much of the VAT you pay to your suppliers on costs such as servicing a mower or buying a new hedge-trimmer.

"If your customers are larger businesses, such as property developers or hotels, you could register voluntarily before you reach this mark," says Emily. This wouldn't be a price increase for them as they will almost certainly be VAT registered themselves and able to reclaim the VAT you charge them. "However, I would recommend avoiding VAT registration for as long as you can if your customers are the general public as it will mean a 20% increase in your prices," she says.

Get insured

There are three principal types of legal liability insurance you are likely to need in this increasingly litigious age, according to Jonathan Leese of insurance broker MFL Professional (*www.m-f-l.co.uk*). He explains:

* *Public liability insurance* protects you against any legal liability you may incur in the course of your business activities for accidental damage to other people's property or accidental injury to persons other than your own employees. For example, if a client were to fall into uncovered footings on-site or trip over a loose paving stone. Make sure any specialist subcontractor has its own PL insurance in place.

* *Employers' liability insurance* is a legal requirement for any firm with employees and includes you as a director of your own limited company. EL protects you against legal liability you may incur for claims made against you by employees for injury or illness sustained in the course of their employment. Like PL insurance, it covers the costs of defending a claim and any damages.

* *Professional indemnity insurance* protects you against legal liability for financial loss incurred by a claimant as a result of your professional negligence. An example would be your liability to a client for the financial consequences of the design of a drainage system not fit for its purpose. Whether or not you need this type of insurance depends on the scope of your activities, but it is essential for firms involved in significant design work.

Other business insurance you may need includes:

★ motor insurance for the use of vehicles in the course of the business (required by law)

★ cover for office and external equipment.

Ask your chosen trade association (see later in this chapter) for approved specialist insurance brokers and take advice from them as to the type and amount of cover you need.

FUNDING

You may be fortunate enough to already own the land for your new nursery like Sue Gray of Damhead Nursery, or have a large and beautiful garden that you have been developing over the years and would now like to open up to the public. Perhaps you have an existing garden building from which you can start to give talks or organise events until your business is ready to expand into new premises.

However, for gardening start-ups that really need additional funding, where can you turn?

★ Family and friends are probably the place to start. It is worth putting something in writing so everyone is absolutely clear on the terms of the loan and when it is to be repaid. This should help pre-empt any misunderstandings.

★ Existing bank overdraft and credit cards – if you have these facilities in place they can be useful in the early days for buying new equipment or helping to tide you over for the first few months until you start generating an income and can pay the money back. *This is a high interest and short-term option.*

Business bank loans are not easy to come by right now, especially for start-ups without a proven track record of previous years' accounts as evidence. National Enterprise Network (*www.national enterprisenetwork.org*) operations manager Rebecca Ireland advises applicants: "Make sure you have the best possible business plan. If your finances are even a little bit vague, or you have a bad credit rating, they will turn you down."

★ If you're aged 18 to 24 and living in England, you can apply for a government-backed start-up loan of up to £2,500 from the Start-Up Loans Company (headed by former Dragon James Caan). Go to *www.startuploans.co.uk*.

★ The Prince's Trust (*www.princes-trust.org.uk*) also offers business support and advice to young people. Its Enterprise Programme has helped more than 78,000 18 to 30-year-olds start their own companies since 1983. It runs four-day courses teaching the basics of business, as well as offering low-interest loans and long-term business mentors.

★ And at the other end of the scale, PRIME (the Prince's Initiative for Mature Enterprise) is aimed at helping those aged over 50 who are unemployed or facing redundancy to become self-employed. It offers practical advice, financial assistance, training and education, organising courses and free networking events. Go to *www.prime.org.uk*.

★ At the time of publication, a New Enterprise Allowance is available for those who have been receiving Jobseeker's Allowance for six months. It's designed to encourage people to set up their own business and get back into work, and involves practical support, a weekly allowance for 26 weeks and a loan of up to £1,000 to get started.

★ Then there are so-called 'business angels' or 'angel investors'. Think *Dragons' Den*. These are wealthy individuals or groups who can provide quite large sums of money (usually a minimum of £10,000) for a stake in your venture and often take a hands-on role in the company. Go to the UK Business Angels Association (*www.bbaa.org.uk*) to find out more.

★ Crowd funding involves big groups raising money online in exchange for small stakes in your start up business or another reward. Crowd-funding platforms include *www.crowdcube.com*, *www.crowdfunder.com* and *www.seedrs.com*.

Local councils often have a business support service and it is worth also contacting them.

A helping hand

1. Find an accountant who, depending on your budget, can take care of everything from company set-up and writing a business plan, to filing annual tax returns and advising on National Insurance payments – not to mention administration of PAYE, VAT and end-of-year accounts. An accountant can also advise what expenses can be offset against tax. Shop around to find someone you like and who is familiar with your kind of business – if possible, go by recommendation.

2. Get a business bank account: it will make it easier to keep track of what is coming in and going out, and make preparing accounts quicker and more straightforward for your accountant, who in turn will need to bill you for less of his or her time. Look for the best deals. Some accounts are free for the first two years and remain so if transactions stay below a certain level.

PLANNING

Generally speaking it is OK planning-wise to work from home. However, having significant numbers of deliveries or customers to your house – with resulting extra traffic or noise – is a different matter.

So if, for example, you're setting up a nursery or an open garden, you may need change-of-use planning permission from your local authority to do so and become liable for paying business rates.

It's something of a fine line, though, and not every nursery or open garden will need it. One senior planning officer explained to me: whether or not planning permission is required for a small, home-grown nursery depends on how much of the garden is to be devoted to the new business, how sales will be taken (online, on-site or a combination of both) and opening times. Similarly, whether or not change of usage is required in opening up your garden to the public depends on the extent to which it becomes a commercial venture and how often it opens.

"Cases are judged on their individual merits. You need to contact your local district council for clarification," she says.

ADVICE

Get advice on these issues and more from:

* GOV.UK (*www.gov.uk*) has information on business premises and rates, as well as tax, setting up, running and funding a company, plus staffing.

* Enterprise Nation, a small business community that helps people start and grow their businesses by putting them in touch with other business owners, providing access to tools and resources and by sharing its own knowledge – via its blog, in books and at live events, including monthly StartUp Saturday workshops. *www.enterprisenation.com*

* The Federation of Small Businesses, which offers free tax and legal advice to members as well as access to free business banking. *www.fsb.org.uk*

* The HMRC website. Go to *www.hmrc.gov.uk/startingup* for advice on registering for National Insurance, tax, VAT and PAYE or call the newly self-employed helpline: 0845 915 4515.

* The National Enterprise Network, which can put you in touch with non-profit making organisations in your area that offer business support, advice and training to pre-start or start-up businesses. *www.nationalenterprisenetwork.org*

* Startups, which is an inspiring, online support service for would-be entrepreneurs packed with information, including profiles of successful ventures and advice on everything from deciding what type of business to start and how to register a company,

through to hiring employees and raising finance, plus business growth. *www.startups.co.uk*

★ And finally, other people doing the job that you would like to do: visit them at markets, fairs, shows, or on-site and chat to them. They're often surprisingly willing to share!

Trade associations

Trade association membership can be invaluable for start-up support, business advice and keeping up-to-date with licensing and legislation, as well as offering networking opportunities.

★ The British Association of Landscape Industries or BALI (*www.bali.co.uk*) is the UK's largest trade association for gardeners, landscapers, garden designers and interior landscape designers. Full membership requires having been established for two years and undergoing a stringent vetting process. The entry point for as-yet-unqualified or sufficiently experienced individuals/businesses is at student or associate level. BALI offers business, technical, training, promotional and legal support, as well as a BALI Finance service (*www.balifinance.co.uk*).

★ Institute of Horticulture (*www.horticulture.org.uk*) members include nurseries/growers, landscapers and people working in botanic/heritage gardens, as well as horticulture students. Membership allows use of the Institute's logo and offers networking opportunities, a continual professional development scheme, a monthly e-newsletter with industry news, updates and events and quarterly publication *The Horticulturist*.

★ Members of the Royal Horticultural Society or RHS (*www.rhs.org.uk*) receive *The Garden* each month, gain free entry to RHS and other selected gardens, get a discount on RHS show tickets, as well as gardening help and advice on anything from plant identification to puzzling pests and diseases, via email or by phone.

★ The Association of Professional Landscapers (*www.landscaper.org.uk*) is part of the larger Horticulture Trades Association (below) and offers student, probationary and full registered membership to garden maintenance, design and construction companies. Full members are expected to have traded for three years-plus, have references to prove it and pass an annual inspection. The APL organises networking meetings, seminars and an annual awards ceremony, has a find-a-landscaper list on its website and a legal and staff advice helpline.

★ The Gardeners Guild (*www.thegardenersguild.co.uk*) is a network of 120 self-employed gardeners and its website is a must-read for anyone looking to set up as a domestic gardener. Membership is just £30 a year and you need at least one nationally-recognised horticultural qualification to join. In return, founder Gary Edwards supplies up-to-date details of legislation, a legal and health-and-safety advice line, as well as a find-a-gardener service.

★ The Horticultural Trades Association (*www.the-hta.org.uk*) is a vast organisation whose members include big growing groups and retailers, as well as smaller independent nurseries. Membership gives access to market information, an advice line and information sheets on the latest regulations, as well as general training and business support.

★ The Society of Garden Designers (*www.sgd.org.uk*) offers student, associate and full accredited membership for garden designers whose work has been rigorously assessed. The SGD organises conferences, training events and local networking groups, including business mentoring for new members. It publishes the monthly *Garden Design Journal* and has produced a standard homeowner's contract. This, and other useful documents, can be found on the SGD website, along with a find-a-designer facility.

★ Not a trade association, exactly, but the Women's Farm & Garden Association (*www.wfga.org.uk*) is designed to bring its keen gardening members together, to make new gardening friends, visit gardens, attend workshops throughout the year and develop gardening skills. It also provides training opportunities (see Chapter 3).

CASE STUDY
MARK YABSLEY
POD GARDEN DESIGN

Mark Yabsley is one half of Pod Garden Design. He and business partner Antonia Young design contemporary gardens for a largely young, professional demographic in and around the London area.

Pod gardens typically feature pale stone and clean lines with grasses and perennial planting. The pair undertake 10–12 design jobs a year, of which they project monitor two or three. They also offer maintenance to former clients to keep Pod gardens looking tip top – a better showcase for their work – as well as a planting service for other designers, plus garden tidies for house sales and a pot-planting service.

Antonia worked in the music industry and Mark as a small business manager for Barclays bank, advising a wide range of existing and start-up ventures on company structure, cash flow and business loans.

"All the time I was helping other people set up their own companies, I wanted to have my own," says Mark, "And I wanted to do something I was passionate about."

Mark was a long-time hobby gardener. The catalyst for his career change was a period of ill health. He took some time off and did some garden maintenance. This was followed by an Open College Network Diploma in garden design at Capel Manor College, where he and Antonia met. And, in 2008, Pod Garden Design was formed.

Their company was founded, as you might expect, on a sound business plan which continues to be reviewed every quarter as their business evolves. Mark and Antonia are equal shareholders in Pod Garden Design Ltd, but their company is not yet VAT-registered as its turnover comes in under the £77,000 mark.

"People's circumstances are different so my recommendation would be to get advice on your company status from GOV.UK or an accountant," Mark says.

Antonia's background means she is perfectly equipped for client liaison and marketing. Mark takes care of the day-to-day accounts. He also lectures at his former college on setting up and running your own business, passing on all he has learnt to the next generation. The design side is shared between the two.

Their company has public liability insurance and employer's liability insurance, of course, though not professional indemnity cover. "Of all the garden designers I speak to there seems to be a 50/50 split on this. It depends on the type and complexity of schemes you are designing," says Mark. "It can be quite an expense." And one, for the moment, he feels Pod doesn't need.

The pair invested £2,500 each into the company by way of repayable directors loans at the outset and all other equipment bought since then has been funded through cash flow. Though they have recently acquired a van each through a lease-purchase agreement. "Even with a one man band a van is important," Mark says.

Ambitious plans for the future include (short term) increased media coverage of themselves as designers and their gardens, (medium term) taking on staff so they can oversee maintenance and leave someone else to do the pruning and the digging and (long term) to make an international name for themselves.

"I know this isn't always practical, but you probably need to spend as much time running the business, doing the admin, bookkeeping, maintaining the website and marketing yourself each week, as you do working in it," Mark says.

And what is his top tip for anyone thinking of running their own gardening business? "Quite simply study, network and then do it," he says.

"Running your own business is not nearly as daunting as you might think."

★ *www.podgardendesign.co.uk*

CASE STUDY
SUE GRAY
DAMHEAD NURSERY

Damhead Nursery sits in windswept countryside on the edge of the Pentland Hills just six miles south of Edinburgh city centre, a handy five minutes in the car from its bypass. Owner Sue Gray specialises in hardy stock which she grows at the nursery to withstand the rigours of the Scottish winter, rather than importing from sunnier climes.

"We want to supply our customers, many of whom live in exposed locations, with plants that are strong and robust and won't keel over in shock at our weather conditions shortly after purchase," she explains.

Sue's range includes native broadleaved and ornamental trees, plus conifers, fruit trees and bushes, climbers and nursery-grown box.

She worked previously as a landscape architect in Edinburgh and was "lucky to have worked on some really interesting projects", among them landscape proposals for new company headquarters, visitor centres for historic buildings and town centre re-development sites.

But Sue felt, after 18 years, that she had moved further and further away from her first love – that of plants. And so, with a five-acre paddock attached to her garden at Damhead "doing very little", she decided it was time for a change.

The nursery is sited on green-belt land, so getting planning permission to build it took three years. Sue was still working at the time, developing her kitchen table-top enterprise in the evenings after work. "I knew, having been in the profession for so long, that the planning process would take time. So I used that time to do my research," she says. The business plan that evolved out of this has been a vital element and Sue goes back to it still, reviewing and revising it as the company develops.

She called in landscape contractors with whom she had worked on previous projects to build the nursery, complete with fencing, irrigation, pathways and plant beds. It opened for business in 2005 and today occupies two acres of the total five-acre site, giving plenty of room for growth. Shrubs, vegetables and bedding plants are grown in a Keder polytunnel, also used for over-wintering young evergreen plants before they go outdoors to harden off. The tunnel has proved to be "worth every penny" as, since it went up, the winters have been particularly tough.

The business is run as a limited company. Sue started her venture part-time – her first customers collected plants from the garden as the nursery was still under construction – but it soon took off and Sue left her old job to run it full-time. This she does with help from assistant manager Euan Girdwood, a horticulturist by training, who looks after customer orders. Office manager Michelle Stewart deals with paperwork and online sales, while Sue runs the business and the nursery's landscape design service. All three job descriptions require a degree of multi-skilling and, between them, they tend to the plants. "We all pitch in. We are usually totally flat out but that's good," Sue says.

Sue's background means she is perfectly positioned to understand what her customers, including architects, landscape designers and contractors, need and want. What started out as a wholesale nursery has since moved into online retail sales, offering free local delivery. And, most recently, after a second lengthy planning procedure to get permission to do so, Damhead now opens to the public for retail sales. "To diversify the business was part of the original plan," Sue says.

Advice came from local start-up organisation Business Gateway Edinburgh (part of *business.scotland.gov.uk*), as well as from enterprising family members who had created a specialist wine store and café in Perthshire from a disused dovecot and cattle shed. Local plant growers and other nurseries helped out too.

But even with this support, and Sue's extensive experience, her new venture has still proved a "steep learning curve" but one that has been worth the effort. Her top tip for anyone looking to set up their own gardening business is:

"Do your groundwork and research. Really take time to look at your marketplace and determine who your key customer type is."

★ *www.damheadnursery.co.uk*

CHAPTER 5

Forming a Company (Practicalities)

W ith the technicalities of running your own gardening business taken care of, let's look at the practicalities.

IN THE BEGINNING

Choose a name

Your business needs a name that gives a good impression and tells people what you do. Some good examples in this book are Architectural Plants, Gardenmakers and Garden Rescue.

Many garden designers, though, choose simply to go under their own name – since it's their personal services they're marketing. James Alexander-Sinclair, for example.

Even if you are a planning to just be a sole trader, it is worth checking that your name isn't already trademarked or registered at Companies House.

The other thing to check is domain names. Sometimes this can reveal businesses with similar names to yours, and may prompt a rethink. Otherwise, it's at this point that you need to register the web addresses you want for your business. Take a look at registering some social media accounts with your name, too. Don't worry about posting anything to them yet; it's just a good idea to secure them as soon as you can.

Establish your identity

Determine your brand identity and the logo that will appear on your headed paper, van, catalogue, signage and/or website. It is worth calling on the services of a graphic designer friend if you have one, or getting the job professionally done.

Jake Judd, creative director of digital and design agency Judd Associates (*www.juddassoc.com*) explains:

"Branding is as important a consideration as any other part of your business because you can project a picture of what you are through your logo. A tree might suggest landscaping; a trowel that you offer a more mechanical service."

Tailor your identity to your target customer.

Get a website

Having a presence online – even if your business exists entirely offline – is a must.

Jake's advice is to choose an address that matches your company name. Failing that, one that includes the service you offer, such as *garden design* or *perennials*. Go for .co.uk if your business is mainly UK-based.

What about design?

"Your website must be clear and engaging. Look at competitors in your area and decide which elements are appropriate to you. Research shows that internet users make up their minds about a website in the blink of an eye, regardless of the quality of the content, or how professional an organisation is," Jake says.

(More on an effective online presence – including appearing high in search engine results, and social media marketing – in Chapter 8.)

Get kitted out

Equipment costs for gardeners are relatively low, and you may already have much of what you need. But don't forget basic maintenance tools and somewhere to keep them, such as a garage or secure shed; the right clothes for the job; and a van/car and trailer for getting around and clearing rubbish. Go to *www.environment-agency.gov.uk* to find out about registering to carry green waste.

Leasing a vehicle (or buying it through hire purchase or a bank loan), rather than buying it outright, means you can spread the cost over an agreed period. It means you don't sink too much of your available funds into one thing – leaving you free to make the day-to-day payments that a business depends on to survive. Just be sure to do the maths first, as high interest rates can sometimes cancel out the benefit. If it's a vehicle you're getting hold of, as long as its a van rather than a car you should be able to claim tax relief.

Conservatory plant specialist Lisa Rawley of Fleur de Lys lists her office, computer, PowerPoint (for client presentations), camera, notebook, tape measure, secateurs and ties as essential equipment costs. "I do have a wonderful trailer like a small horsebox which is essential for larger projects," she says. "And a pot mover, work boots and all kinds of gardening equipment."

Similarly, most garden designers and coaches will have a drawing board, camera, computer and ample reference books from their studies. The program Vectorworks Landmark, for producing computer-drawn plans, costs around £1,500 plus VAT. Garden coach Alison Marsden has a 30m tape, spirit level and basic laser level in her kit, plus a projector for workshops and talks.

Open garden and nursery start-up costs depend on what you already have in terms of infrastructure and planting, and what you hope to achieve. Maintenance equipment, greenhouses/polytunnels, trollies for moving plants plus pots and compost, with ultimately some kind of head office building, parking and a tearoom, may well be on the list. "Disregarding rent or land purchase, a small nursery with plastic tunnels and using mains water for irrigation and secondhand equipment could be started with a very modest budget," says Angus White of Architectural Plants.

Designer Denise Cadwallader advises:

> "Don't spend money you haven't got. Let your business grow steadily and reinvest the money that comes in. If you go out and blow £10,000 you are likely to fall flat on your face."

Suppliers

Having good, reliable suppliers will help you do your job much faster and more easily. Setting up a trade account with them means you receive an invoice for payment within 28 days rather than paying upfront. You should also be charged at a lower trade (rather than retail) price. But do be aware that the price they give you will be ex-VAT, so you will need to add 20% when working out your budget. Otherwise you could be in for a nasty shock!

Whatever college you choose to study at will no doubt provide you with a list of local suppliers relevant to your chosen area of gardening, and in time you will build up contacts of your own. However, here is a round-up of some of my favourites and those recommended by some of the gardeners, nursery owners and designers profiled in this book . . .

Pots

Pots and Pithoi (*www.potsandpithoi.com*) – a vast selection of Cretan pots, urns, water features and jars

Pret a Pot (*www.pret-a-pot.co.uk*) – contemporary pots and planters for indoors and outdoors

Whichford Pottery (*www.whichfordpottery.com*) – a wide range of British handmade pots

Plants

Hortus Loci (*www.hortusloci.co.uk*) – wholesale plant nursery for trees, shrubs and perennials from across the UK and Europe, plus pots, stone, lighting and fencing

Coblands (*www.coblands.co.uk*) – well-established nursery with wholesale division supplying gardeners, designers and contactors nationwide

Orchard Dene (*www.orcharddene.co.uk*) – much written about Oxfordshire-based wholesale nursery for hardy perennials, ferns and grasses

Specialist nurseries

Architectural Plants (*www.architecturalplants.com*) – profiled in Chapter 1, specialising in exotic, evergreen plants

David Austin Roses (*www.davidaustin.com*) – name synonymous with English roses

Langley Boxwood Nurseries (*www.boxwood.co.uk*) – Hampshire-based box specialist

Tree nurseries

Griffin Nurseries (*www.griffinnurseries.co.uk*) – specimen plant producer specialising in trees, shrubs, hedging, pleaching and topiary

Majestic Trees (*www.majestictrees.co.uk*) – Hertfordshire-based nursery selling mature and semi-mature trees

Tendercare Nurseries (*www.tendercare.co.uk*) – nursery stocking specimen trees and plants for instant effect

Furniture

Encompass Co (*www.encompassco.com*) – super-sleek minimalist European outdoor furniture

Gaze Burvill (*www.gazeburvill.com*) – timeless and beautifully-crafted oak outdoor furniture

Gloster (*www.gloster.com*) – higher-end teak, metal and woven furniture

Fencing, decking, sheds, etc

AVS Fencing (*www.avsfencing.co.uk*) – fencing and decking specialist

Irrigation and lighting

City Irrigation (*www.cityirrigation.co.uk*) – Large-scale supplier (also designer and installer if needed) of irrigation systems

Lighting for Gardens (*www.lightingforgardens.com*) – supplier of garden and exterior lighting

Waterwell (*www.waterwell.co.uk*) – supply, installation and maintenance of irrigation and lighting supplies

Bulbs

Walkers (*www.bulbs.co.uk*) – UK's biggest bulb supplier to the trade

Equipment (to hire)

HSS Hire (*www.hss.com*) – nationwide chain hiring out a wide range of garden and building equipment

Hire Station (*www.hirestation.co.uk*) – again, a nationwide hire chain

Mayday Plant Hire (*www.maydayplanthire.co.uk*) – plant and tool hire company for in and around the London area

Equipment (to buy)

Countrywide Farmers (*www.countrywidefarmers.co.uk*) – 53-store-strong stockist of gardening tools, machinery and sundries

Stihl (*www.stihl.co.uk*) – recommended brand of lawnmowers and power tools; check out their site for stockists

Tools

Bacho (*www.bahco.com*) – gardening tools manufacturer. Go to website for stockist details

Felco (*www.worldoffelco.co.uk*) – the gardeners' secateurs of choice

Niwaki (*www.niwaki.com*) – founder Jake Hobson sells Japanese tripod ladders and tools for precision pruning

Compost, topsoil, gravel and turf

AHS (*www.ahs-ltd.co.uk*) – supplies and delivers bark, mulch, compost and soil improver

Rockinghams (*www.rockinghams.co.uk*) – London area supplier of turf, topsoil, mulch and compost

Rowlawn (*www.rowlawn.co.uk*) – Nationwide turf and topsoil supplier for retail and trade

Nursery buildings

Clovis Lande (*www.clovislande.co.uk*) – greenhouses, polytunnels and polycarbonate glazing

Keder (*www.kedergreenhouse.co.uk*) – high specification UK-based manufacturer and supplier of greenhouses

Northern Polytunnels (*www.northernpolytunnels.co.uk*) – for polytunnels, fruitcages and raised beds

Stone

CED (*www.ced.ltd.uk*) – supplier of natural stone paving and cobbles

London Stone (*www.londonstone.com*) – again, supplier of a wide range of stone including sandstone, slate, granite and Portland stone

Marshalls (*www.marshalls.co.uk*) – large-scale supplier of paving, block paving and natural stone

Horticultural sundries

Green-tech (*www.green-tech.co.uk*) – large-scale supplier of grass seed, fertiliser, soils, tree planting sundries, etc.

East Riding Horticulture (*www.eastridinghorticultureltd.co.uk*) – trolleys, wheelbarrows, pots, polytunnels, labels and ties, etc.

Fargro (*www.fargro.co.uk*) – for fogging equipment, disinfectants, insecticides, shading, etc.

LBS Horticultural Supplies (*www.lbsbuyersguide.co.uk*) – for a wide range of horticultural, landscaping and irrigation supplies.

Establish your pricing

Set your price for plants, an hourly rate for planting/maintenance/design work, or your entry fees. If a gardener or a designer, work out how you will cover your travel time and costs. If a nursery, establish your delivery charge. If your customers include commercial gardeners, designers and other nurseries, decide whether you will offer them a trade discount. And establish how you'll receive payment: by cash, cheque, credit card or a combination of all three.

Gary Edwards of the Gardeners Guild recommends standing order payments for garden maintenance work, or using online banking and direct bank transfers which are generally free. "It means fast payment and clients not having to keep cash in the house," he says.

Nurseries and open gardens selling significant quantities of plants will need to make the necessary banking arrangements to take debit and credit card payments, and require an internet merchant account to make online sales. (Speak to your bank to find out more.)

Payment terms

While domestic gardeners and coaches are likely to be paid more or less on the spot, gardeners working for commercial clients could find themselves waiting up to 90 days, depending on their clients' payment terms, though this is something you may be able to negotiate. Designers need to decide if they will ask for staged payments throughout the project to aid cash flow, and how soon after invoicing they expect the money.

Nurseries and open gardens will be investing time and money at the outset, reaping the rewards of plant and entrance sales often much later. If you are working to a tight budget, minimise outlay by growing your business slowly, hiring equipment or buying second hand where appropriate, recycling pots and other materials whenever possible and propagating new plants from your existing stock.

Paperwork perfection

Get the correct, headed paperwork (which should include your contact details, as well as VAT and company information where applicable) – it looks much more professional.

Organisations such as BALI and the SGD can help with the appropriate documents for your business, including, for example, terms and conditions, contracts and building specifications. As landscape designer Jonnie Wake explains:

"Having the correct contractual documents will not only offer a degree of financial protection but will also reassure potential clients that you operate professionally."

DAY TO DAY

Seasonal rhythm

Forward planning, establishing a seasonal rhythm and using quiet times to get on top of stock-taking, marketing and accounts will really help spread your workload throughout the year. You can also anticipate the peaks and troughs of your cash flow this way and plan your business expenditure and personal finances accordingly.

For gardeners, summer lawn-cutting and hedge-trimming gives way to autumn leaf clearance and pruning before winter repairs and maintenance and spring planting and tidy ups. Winter months can be lean, so offering an annual contract can help stabilise your income year-round, says Gary Edwards of The Gardeners Guild.

For garden designers, autumn/winter is a good time for getting structural elements of the garden built. You can use spring for planting (hopefully giving plants a chance to get established before the weather warms up) and summer for planning – as that's when clients are thinking of their gardens most. August and Christmas, when things go quiet, are good times to take a well-deserved break.

Some independent nurseries such as Marchants Hardy Plants in Chapter 6 shut up shop from October to March, as their plant palette simply isn't suited to the winter months. Yeo Valley's Organic Garden also closes for essential maintenance.

Bookkeeping

Keep on top of filing invoices and bank statements, as well as receipts for items purchased for work, a record of your mileage plus utility and phone bills. These receipts can be given to your accountant and off-set against tax. Make it company policy to pay your bills on time and to invoice straightaway – if you don't invoice, you won't get paid.

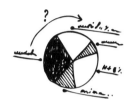

Business software solutions company Sage (*www.sage.co.uk*) has accountancy packages which allow you to prepare your own VAT and tax returns (as well as manage cash flow, payroll, etc).

Accountant Emily Coltman says:

"Not keeping your books up-to-date can result in a lot of problems, not least because you won't know how much profit and cash your business is earning and you could risk spending money on a project that won't cover its costs."

She recommends having a filing system, be that the old-fashioned way with a set of lever-arch files, or a system of scanning your records to your computer.

Designer Denise Cadwallader says:

"So much of my time is spent not designing but invoicing, organising my maintenance schedule, going to see jobs and quoting, sourcing and ordering materials and plants, keeping on top of day-to-day accounting as well as marketing – of which I still don't do nearly enough!"

Finger on the pulse

Keep up-to-date with gardening issues, trends and new legislation. Good sources for this include interiors and gardening magazines such as *Country Living*, as well as specialist industry titles *The Garden*, *The Garden Design Journal*, *The Horticulturist* and *Horticulture Week*, plus broadsheet gardening supplements. Online gardening forum *www.landscapejuicenetwork.com* is useful reading and a place of topical debate.

Take advantage of workshops and lectures organised by the trade association relevant to you. Go to events and flower shows. The Horticultural Trades Association organises the HTA National Plant Show (*www.national plantshow.co.uk*) each year to showcase British plant suppliers.

Likewise GLEE, The Garden Retail Show (*www.gleebirmingham.co.uk*), is held every September at the NEC. The LANDSCAPE Show at Olympia, London, is for landscape designers, architects and contractors (*www.landscapeshow.co.uk*). The RHS also puts on inspiring talks and nursery tours all over the UK, right throughout the year. Go to the website *www.rhs.org.uk* to find out more.

CASE STUDY
Louise Cummins and Caroline De Lane Lea
Gardenmakers

Louise Cummins and Caroline De Lane Lea – aka the Gardenmakers – met studying for their one-year garden design diplomas at the English Gardening School (*englishgardeningschool.co.uk*). Louise worked for an international property firm before a ten-year career break to have children. Caroline was fresh from 15 years at the educational arm of auction house Christie's. Both graduated with distinctions in the summer of 2003 and started up their own garden design businesses.

They began as self-employed sole traders operating under the same banner. But as work built up they formalised the arrangement and set up a partnership, splitting everything down the middle.

The pair sat down in the early planning stages to discuss marketing and promotion. They wanted to create a logo that was simple, timeless and would work for both the website and the stationery. They called on the services of a graphic designer friend who they repaid in design advice and plants. And, while the website has evolved over the years, it has remained the same at its core.

Though Louise is based in Surrey and Caroline in central London, they get together regularly to discuss projects, marketing, business development and to work on designs. They divide work, appointing a lead designer to each project. While Caroline functions as company secretary, Louise takes a lead on marketing. "Working as a team is much more time efficient," she says.

They have become much more selective about which projects they take on over the years, and are careful to manage these so they don't have too many at the same stage of development at any one time. Their work is a mix of small inner city courtyards, big rural gardens and large suburban plots in London and the surrounding Home Counties, and they like the variety that projects of different sizes brings.

Caroline explains the initial process. Like most garden designers, this starts with a chat on the phone to gain an outline of the client's needs, followed by a visit to the garden to discuss the project further.

"This first meeting is crucial for establishing the client's wish list," she says. "In some cases they will have a very clear idea of what they want, in others it may be an open book. It takes a while to develop the skills to adjust to each different situation and respond accordingly."

"If a client tells us they want a terrace for outdoor eating and entertaining, with a water feature and bespoke pergola, but only has a budget of £5,000, then we might have to help them gain a more realistic picture of likely costs."

Following this meeting, a proposal is sent out as soon as possible, providing the client with full details as to how the project might be approached. The design stages and other aspects of the garden redevelopment are outlined, along with a fee proposal, business terms and contract.

Having worked together for almost ten years now, the Gardenmakers have settled into a comfortable rhythm, pacing their work and planning ahead to counter the seasonal nature of gardening work. Planting takes place from late February through to mid-June and then again through October, November and December. Gardens are built throughout the year, weather permitting, but January tends to be a quieter month and a good time to get on with design work and filing. "Juggling all aspects of the job can be tricky as it's not just about sitting in an office doing design," explains Louise. "You are running a business and a lot of time is spent on site visits, meeting clients, contractors, sourcing products and plants." The partnership model works well for the pair – the belief that two heads are better than one.

Their top tip is this:

> "Remember you are running a business and from the outset you need to wear a business hat. If you don't have previous experience, then get some with another garden designer or volunteer in a larger design practice to gain an understanding of all aspects of the job. Go to as many seminars, trade shows, nursery visits, conferences and talks as possible and network like mad before you make a start."

★ *www.garden-makers.co.uk*

CASE STUDY

ALAN SHIPP
NATIONAL COLLECTION OF HYACINTHS

Alan Shipp is the proud owner the National Collection of Hyacinths. His collection totals 180 varieties and is the largest in the world. Many of these are rare, dating as far back as 1794, and came into Alan's hands from the former Soviet Union via Rita Raziulyte, a former flower field station worker in Lithuania, who tracked him down. It was a moment he describes as "like finding a long lost masterpiece in somebody's attic".

He describes himself as a "keen gardener", though dedication to his two-acre hyacinth field means his own garden doesn't get nearly the attention it deserves. Alan's background is in farming (wheat, sugar beet and potatoes) but, back in the 1980s, he decided to try his hand at a higher value crop. It was a moment of pure serendipity that decided what that crop should be. He was lifting the 100 hyacinth bulbs he had planted in his garden the previous year and missed one which rolled under a bush. When he discovered it a year later, slugs had eaten away most of the baseplate (i.e. the bottom of the bulb) exposing the scales around the outside and the base where small bulbs had developed.
      "The principle of commercial propagation," Alan says.

Armed with 23 questions on all things from where to buy planting stock and methods of propagating, to national consumption of hyacinth bulbs, he contacted environmental and rural development consultancy ADAS who sent a representative out and gave Alan a three-hour briefing. With this, "50 or 60" varieties from the former National Collection of Hyacinths when it folded, a further 200 kilos of more common varieties bought from Holland and a natural aptitude for growing, Alan set out on his new venture.

He describes himself as "semi-retired", though in reality Alan works up to ten hours a day, seven days a week, starting in January when he sprays his fields to kill off any overwintered weeds so the bulbs come up through clean soil. The last weekend in March is the date for the National Hyacinth Collection open weekend, which attracts around 400–500 visitors, depending on the level of national media coverage that year (in 2004 it was 1,077). People come from across the country to admire the collection and place orders.

The lead-up to this is a busy time, with Alan weeding and removing stray or diseased bulbs. Alan produces a single sheet bulb list of 30–40 varieties and a separate order form, taking orders on the day or later via email or post. He keeps the fields weed-free until mid-late June when the bulbs are harvested, cleaned and graded. Sold bulbs are dispatched in August, when customers can come and collect in person. Bulbs kept to be grown on for the following year are replanted from September to mid-November.

Work is done the old fashioned way at the National Collection of Hyacinths. Save ten hours' mechanised planting and harvesting of mass varieties each year, Alan plants, lifts and propagates by hand. Further, he doesn't have a sales website of his own, though the open day is listed on the Plant Heritage website (*www.nccpg.com*). Rare varieties are sent to US heritage bulb retailer Old House Gardens (*www.oldhousegardens.com*) for which Alan needs to issue his bulbs with a Plant Passport for export. But this can only be done after the plant health inspectorate, on the lookout for the potato cyst nematode, has examined the bulbs first growing in the field and then once harvested and dried. (No such

restrictions apply when selling in the UK, though this may change in the next few years as Plant Passports are rolled out across all commercial plant sales.) A bit like the weeding, this business – and the financial side – is something Alan makes sure he keeps under control.

Though Alan works until dusk most evenings, at the age of 74 he doesn't feel the financial pressure to maximise his output, which goes some way to explaining why even his rarest varieties are sold for just £1.

> "I'm trying to discipline myself to charge more and I know I must. But for me, it is the satisfaction of saving something from extinction and distributing it to be grown around the country. And you cannot put a price on that."

His advice?

> "I think the most important thing is to be sure you have a customer base. It's no good unless you have a place to sell things and that determines your production."

CHAPTER 6

Establishing a Client Base

So, you've completed your training, formed your company, developed a brand, got kitted out and insured. You are a proper, bona fide business. Now all you need are some customers . . .

Family and friends

Family and friends (and *their* friends) in need of horticultural guidance – be that advice, a hedge-clipping service, new plants or a complete new garden look – are a good place to start. Most new gardening businesses begin this way and it should kick-start referrals for other jobs.

You could offer your services free of charge or at reduced, so-called *mates' rates* to get photos of completed projects for your website and portfolio. This is also a useful way of refining your working practice before launching yourself to a wider public.

A word of caution, though – my own experience is that you can, quite soon, start to feel taken advantage of. Do make sure your expenses are covered at the very least, and that you start charging properly for your services as soon as you can.

Moira Farnham is an experienced garden designer and co-founder of the Garden Design School (*www.garden designschool.co.uk*). Her advice is to make use of your existing contacts, "whether you were a City high flier, a mum at home or working in a completely different field. Tell people what you are doing and don't underestimate how fascinated they will be by your change of career."

These people may then tell their friends, who will come to you as recommendations. "That way, you leapfrog any kind of paid-for advertising, which is much less beneficial than people expect," she says.

Local magazines and noticeboards

Parish magazines and local newsagents' noticeboards are another good way to start building a loyal, local customer base and the advertising costs are minimal. My local *Funtington Parish Magazine*, for example, charges just £40 a year for a small, black-and-white box ad and is distributed to 450 largely affluent households within a three-mile radius – which means not travelling far for work. Local newsagents and farm shops often allow you to pin your well-designed business card or leaflet up for around £1 a week.

"School magazines can also work well," says Moira. "Offer to speak at your local WI group. I gave a talk at a local gardening club when I first started. I was terrified and it was a horrible experience at the time. But you have got to put yourself outside of your comfort zone."

Leaflet drop

You could also try an old-fashioned leaflet drop to selected households and businesses – including estate agents, lettings agents, businesses new to the area, big gardens owned by busy professionals, time-strapped parents with young children, and so on.

Landscape designer Jonnie Wake cites the example of a friend who cannily typed: "I specialise in pruning wisterias," and dropped this through the letterbox of every smart house he could find in his select part of London with a wisteria in the garden. In

January/February and again in June/July each year (wisteria pruning time) he works flat out, employing two or three extra men at any one time.

Auctions and charities

You could donate your services to a local good cause and offer to clear, mow, tidy, redesign or supply plants to a garden belonging to a local charity, animal sanctuary or school.

You will be busy, gaining valuable experience, pictures for your website and doing something worthwhile, as well as generating new leads and possibly even local newspaper coverage – if you get in touch with the news desk and let it know.

Or how about putting your garden services up for auction at a local school or charity event and have people actually bid for your expertise?

Farmers' markets and local shows

What about taking a stand at a local show or farmers' market and selling plants or giving out leaflets and other information telling people what you do?

There are plenty of events to choose from, from local school fetes to regional shows. My local show is the Garden Show (*www.thegardenshowonline.com*), which runs at Stansted Park in Hampshire, Firle Place in East Sussex and Loseley Park in Surrey each year, and where a 10 × 10 foot stand costs around £180.

There are also increasingly popular weekly farmers' markets selling food, plants and showcasing local businesses up and down the country each week.

Show garden at RHS events

What about designing a show garden at an RHS event (*www.rhs.org.uk/shows-events*)? Each year you have:

* RHS Flower Show Tatton Park in Cheshire

* RHS Chelsea Flower Show and RHS Hampton Court Palace Flower Show in London

* RHS Show Cardiff

* BBC Gardeners' World Live in Birmingham (*www.bbcgardenersworldlive.com*).

So there are plenty of events in different locations to choose from. Go to the RHS website to apply.

These shows are a great way of making contact with the landscape contractor who will build your garden (and to observe how this works), as well as the nurseries that will supply your plants, fellow designers at the show with whom you can swap stories and compare notes, and the press who will be on the look-out for bold designs, inspiring planting schemes and new names to write about. Many colleges encourage students to display at RHS events: it is a fast track to pictures for your portfolio. This was the strategy adopted, with great success, by the young designer in our next profile, Hugo Bugg.

Word of mouth

Meanwhile, get out and about and talk to people. It was while getting her final college garden design project printed that Moira Farnham got her first new lead. The lady next to her in the queue at the printing shop said: "I think my husband would be interested – he's a landscaper."

Moira did a little work for him; she also went to see a "house builder I vaguely knew. I offered to design show gardens for him for next to nothing in exchange for him promoting my services," she says.

In time, of course, and provided your pricing is right, you are offering the right kind of service and doing a good job, your name will spread, work will start to come through word-of-mouth referral and your customer base will grow. You can see this process in the profile of Graham Gough of Marchant's Hardy Plants later in the chapter.

For now, let's hear from Hugo Bugg on how to get your first job . . .

CASE STUDY
Hugo Bugg
Garden designer

Hugo Bugg landed his first commission – to work on a £22m sustainable housing development in Cornwall – at his graduation show. He has since built four show gardens, won three RHS medals, been hailed RHS Young Designer of the Year 2010, lectured at Grand Designs Live and The LANDSCAPE Show and taught at the prestigious Inchbald School of Design.

In a very short time, he has achieved rather a lot – and seems the ideal person to speak to about getting your first job. His plan was to "work as fast as I could and to win as many medals as possible", to make a name in the industry. And it's worked. Four years out of college, Hugo's current commissions include two large, private gardens in Dorset and a roof-top garden in Regents Park, central London.

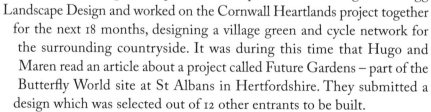

He studied Garden Design at University College Falmouth, where he met future business partner Maren Hallenga. The pair teamed up to form Hallenga and Bugg Landscape Design and worked on the Cornwall Heartlands project together for the next 18 months, designing a village green and cycle network for the surrounding countryside. It was during this time that Hugo and Maren read an article about a project called Future Gardens – part of the Butterfly World site at St Albans in Hertfordshire. They submitted a design which was selected out of 12 other entrants to be built.

"It was a fantastic start but we were just so busy, we really didn't have time to think about it," Hugo says. "There were so many things we had to learn about, such as how to build and where to source materials and plants."

The following year, Hugo and Maren gave a seminar at Grand Designs Live to an audience of 70 at the NEC, on the subject of combining formal and informal design. Were they daunted? "Yes, it was very daunting as it was our first, but Maren and I had been invited to 10 Downing Street that evening and I was more concerned we would be late," Hugo says. This talk, publicity generated by Future Gardens and other media exposure, led to the commission of Hallenga and Bugg's first private garden design work.

Hugo got stuck in with characteristic gusto. Undeterred by running four different projects simultaneously – and hundreds of miles apart – he spent as much time as possible on-site, observing the contractors and learning about how to build terraces and walls.

Maren left the company at the beginning of 2010 to work full-time on a family charity, leaving Hugo to re-establish himself as simply Hugo Bugg Landscapes. He did this by building another show garden, this time at RHS Flower Show Tatton Park (a last-minute decision, designing the plans and submitting them within a week). RHS sponsorship for the garden totalled £12,000, which left Hugo £4,000 short to build the garden he really wanted. Not prepared to compromise, he and a dedicated team camped at the site for a month and built the garden themselves to save money.

Their effort paid off and Hugo's Albert Dock Garden gained him a gold medal and Best in Show. But now he couldn't afford to dismantle it. So he contacted local schools and offered the garden, free of charge, to anyone who could take it away. It went to a secondary school in Dorset in the end, generating goodwill and further publicity along the way.

Show gardens have proved a powerful advertising tool for Hugo, getting him noticed and – while not necessarily showcasing the kind of scheme a client might want in their own garden – providing him with a portfolio to show potential customers. Lately, his focus has been on developing his business, the Hugo Bugg brand and private work. The fact that he has no family ties means he can dedicate himself wholeheartedly to the task. "I throw myself at everything and am not too worried about earning loads of money just yet," he says.

His advice to anyone starting out now is:

> "Don't say no to anything. I graduated in garden design but have taken on anything related that has come my way – graphic design, website design – and it has led to garden projects further down the line."

★ *www.hugobugg.com*

CASE STUDY
Graham Gough
Marchants Hardy Plants

You are unlikely to come across this independent nursery by accident. Tucked down a secluded lane in East Sussex, Marchants Hardy Plants doesn't shout about its presence with signs to direct passing trade from the nearby road. Once inside, there are no distracting horticultural sundries. This is a place where plants reign supreme: a nirvana for gardeners looking for inspiration, advice and well-grown plants.

Marchants Hardy Plants is very much an independent nursery. It is open seven months of the year, from mid-March to mid-October. The emphasis is on owner Graham Gough's four favourites – agapanthus, kniphofia, miscanthus and sedum – but walking round the garden there is a long list of others. Virtually all the plants for sale here are grown in the nursery and Graham propagates most of them himself.

"Our style is so much geared to March–October that we would have to pander to people's tastes to remain open year-round, and I am not prepared to do that," he explains. There is a detailed website listing what's on sale, but Marchants doesn't sell online. To buy plants, customers must make the journey to the village of Laughton, East Sussex themselves.

Even before you have turned into the car park it is evident the nursery has been shaped by a gardener with tremendous artistic flair. The boundary hedge floats in the air, formed from trees that were laid at two metres high, allowing views through into the garden. Inside, curving paths lure you through tall, generous plantings of grasses and perennials woven between fine trees and shrubs. Throughout, the overall design and detail are immensely pleasing, and there is much to emulate.

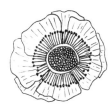

Graham was a young music student when he took on work as a jobbing gardener to help make ends meet. Hungry to learn more, he worked for 16 years at Washfield Nursery with Elizabeth Strangman, an inspirational plantswoman who specialised in woodland plants. Time passed, Graham's knowledge grew and he realised the moment had come to look for his own nursery. And so he left, with Elizabeth's blessing and her mailing list which was to form the basis of Marchants' customer base. "We culled it quite efficiently to people in the south east and on our first mailing contacted the first few hundred. It has expanded thereafter because of our reputation," Graham says.

He attributes the nursery's success to his sound plant knowledge. "We have never, ever advertised," he says. "Word travels quickly in a small place." Typical customers are really keen plantspeople who know about gardening. "We are not exactly austere, but we are not that user friendly. You would have to know about plants to understand our catalogue," Graham says. Much of their business is repeat business, and Marchants treads a fine line here between friendly customer service that keeps people coming back and being too familiar. "We have one lady who comes to us six times a year and spends £30 to £40 each time. I would rather that than a one-off big hit. It's more gentle on the business," he says.

Graham recognised and harnessed the power of the press early on, favouring the free exposure that PR provides over advertising. "I'm not keen on advertising. It has always seemed so random," he says. So two years after opening, he contacted *Gardens Illustrated* magazine who came, photographed and put Marchants on the front cover of their September issue. "Looking back at the photos we were not really ready – but that set us up. The knock-on effect was enormous." The nursery is beautifully-maintained and photogenic, ensuring a steady stream of newspaper and magazine exposure ever since. "We are good to look at and photographers love it. I am very particular that plants don't go out with weeds," he says.

The work involved for Graham and partner Lucy Goffin, who is a textile designer, to generate enough money to live well is a huge manual task for the nursery alone. So Graham also gives talks and lectures, not only to promote the nursery and build its customer base, but to add further income. Some groups visit the nursery as a result, while some book a talk as a result of a visit to the nursery. "I charge quite a lot for this as I couldn't make a living from growing alone. You have to do add-ons," Graham says. These include propagation classes, teaching, consultancy and planting design.

Graham's tip for anyone looking to run their own gardening business is this:

"Nurture and look after your customers and they'll keep on coming back."

★ *www.marchantshardyplants.co.uk*

CHAPTER 7

Building a Network

T he next step in growing your gardening business is to get networking and develop the valuable connections that will help you do your job better and get more work.

YOUR NETWORK

As well as your inner circle of family and friends who can help out with advice and practical support, your network should include some of the following ...

Satisfied customers

Satisfied customers are a source of repeat business. They can also be called on for a reference if you need it. They will (hopefully) recommend your gardening school, nursery, gardening or design services to others.

Social network followers

Followers on Facebook and/or Twitter can help spread the news of your fantastic new open garden or nursery. A 'Join Us on Facebook' (or Twitter) link on your website, business card, invoice or leaflet helps prompt customers (existing and potential) to connect with you

online. And once they've connected, all their friends and followers are now one-step closer to you. Post good content and you'll find your followers being your best spokespeople, sharing your news for free.

For an example of how powerful this can be, look at Jimi Blake in Chapter 2. He has a Facebook page for his Hunting Brook Gardens and updates the page regularly. He took photographs of fields of spectacular bright blue *Meconopsis* 'Lingholm' poppies at his garden and posted them onto the page where the pictures, unsurprisingly, generated great interest. This, in turn, brought around 100 visitors to come and see the fields for themselves, and to buy poppies at €8 each from the Hunting Brook Gardens nursery.

Fellow businesses

Your network should include complimentary local businesses whose specialist services you might need and who you know you can call on to do a good job. These might include gardeners, designers, tree surgeons, water engineers, lighting specialists, surveyors and landscape contractors. You could source these through recommendation, websites such as Checkatrade (*www.checkatrade.com*) which will give you a customer score, as well as through representative trade bodies such as BALI. Hopefully, in time, this will become a reciprocal arrangement and they will call on you too.

Landscape designer Jonnie Wake's network, 20 years in the building, means he has a pool of skilled craftspeople whose work he knows well and can trust. "It is important to have contractors you know are good and with whom you have a sound working relationship," he says. "Then you understand how fast, accurate and skilled they are." Building this network was "trial and error" in the beginning and, having once been let down by a subcontractor (a costly incident), he now checks people out "very carefully" before they are added to his list.

Your network should also include complimentary local businesses through which you might actually get work. These could include architects, house developers, sales and letting agents (great sources of garden tidy-up jobs) as well as landscape designers looking for someone to maintain their clients' gardens or somewhere local to buy plants.

Gardeners Guild founder Gary Edwards explains that much gardeners' work comes this way. "Look for businesses that can recommend you to others," he says. Gary's first gardening job, the maintenance contract for a block of flats, came through a former work colleague. Through that, Gary was awarded maintenance of the neighbouring block. The owner of one of the flats there ran a facilities management company and, through him, Gary gained two more contracts. Thus one single job led to three more.

Suppliers

Suppliers you use – of plants, pots, gardening equipment and turf – may be able to recommend your company to their own customers, with a card at their till or a link on their website through to yours. Forming good quality links from your website to others also helps with search engine optimisation – in other words getting your website to the top of search engine results pages.

Fellow professionals

Your network should also include fellow gardening professionals, perhaps like-minded people you studied with and can call on for advice, an extra pair of hands if you've got too much work on, assistance with a difficult job or even holiday cover. When I started researching this book, it was my old contacts, those from the English Gardening School and magazine articles previously written, that I called first.

Existing networks

Take advantage, too, of existing networks, especially at the outset of your new career, including those of local horticultural societies and the national trade bodies listed in Chapter 4 – many of which organise national awards, annual conferences and local cluster group meetings for that very purpose. These can be a great boost to your contacts book and morale. Check out more general local business networks too – these involve meeting other business people in your area, usually over breakfast or lunch, and will hopefully generate new leads.

New contacts

And finally, get out and about and develop new contacts of your own. Talk to people confidently about your business. Carry a card and tell people what you do. You never know who you might meet, even in the course of a trip to the shops or the school run, or what that might lead to . . .

Landscape designer Jonnie Wake says: "It is a brutal fact of life that getting work is as much about who you know as what you know." His advice, if you don't have those connections, is to get out there and forge them. "You need your headed paper and at the very least an online business card (a webpage with some pictures and a brief outline of what you do). Then start phoning architects, interior designers and property developers, to list just a few targets." Jonnie says be honest, say you are trying to build relationships and go and meet these people. "Set aside a day a week to do so," he says.

Garden designer Moira Farnham agrees.

"I am based in the south east of England which is heavily populated with people earning good incomes. But, while there is plenty of work around, this is not spread evenly, and you have to be hungry to earn your share. It's not just about talent. It's also about strategising. You've got to have a plan and you've got to actually get out there and find work."

CASE STUDY
GILL CHAMBERLAIN
GARDEN RESCUE

It would be true to say that Gill Chamberlain, owner of Garden Rescue, has built her entire business on brilliant networking. Gill offers what she describes as a roving head gardener service – that is to say she manages the planting, on-going maintenance and development of large country gardens and small estates – and her network extends beyond satisfied clients to

landscape contractors, garden designers and nurseries. She also lectures and has written for *The Horticulturist*. Affability is company policy, as is paying invoices on time and Gill makes a point of putting people in touch who might benefit one another.

> "You get a reputation for being helpful and having a good network that way. And then people will come to you as a matter of course," she says.

This approach means Gill has never needed to advertise as all her work comes through word of mouth and her schedule is packed, right through the year, save two weeks over Christmas and in August. "There is a whole circle of us who work together. It's like a family. If I need anything I can pick up the phone and they will be there instantly," she says.

Gill traded her life in senior management at an international computer networking company for that of horticulture student at Writtle College (*www.writtle.ac.uk*) 15 years ago. She spent a year there, before going to work at Cambridge Botanic Gardens (*www.botanic.cam.ac.uk*). Knowing she wanted to do something in gardening but not thinking of herself as a designer, Gill spotted a gap in the market somewhere between garden designer and garden labourer for a knowledgeable, upscale lady gardener, one who "didn't dig", but who really knew her plants. "Someone who knew how to rejuvenate a herbaceous border and could prune a rose without giving it a haircut," she says.

On graduating she realised she "had no contacts" and spent the next three years rectifying this. She attended lectures and garden shows, going up and talking to the guest speaker or show-garden designer at the end and offering her services. "It was just about having the brass to go and talk to people," she says. "They could always say no."

But invariably they didn't, and she soon started helping out with show gardens and assisting designers on bigger planting projects. Her hunch was confirmed and Gill soon realised that while a good proportion of these designers were experts at reorganising space and creating atmosphere, they "didn't necessarily know their plants or what to do with them once they were in the ground and began to develop and mature". It is her belief that there is still a big potential market here, for people who really know their planting and can manage a garden project from the beginning right through to the end.

> "People like me need good designers, they are the keystone, but equally designers need us to take on their designs and turn them into beautiful sustainable gardens."

Her big break came when a new client, a friend of a friend, called and "told me I was doing their garden. It wasn't a request," Gill says; so she redesigned the planting for their three-acre plot. These same clients have since moved to a 35-acre estate and here Gill has overseen the lot, from organising the felling of dangerous trees, to finding the right person to metal edge the drive, arranging onsite parking for big summer parties and dealing with drought restrictions. "Really everything outside the house which doesn't come under the builder's remit comes under mine," she says.

Gill's client list, of which she has ten to 12 main regulars (all of which can be characterised as having large country gardens with gardeners to maintain them), has been built up by just such repeat business and friend-of-friend referrals.

> "Networking is an art and I have been accused of talking to anyone," she says. "But you never know when you might come across someone who could be useful, even if it takes years to pay off."

And what is Gill's advice to anyone starting their own gardening business now?

> "Be absolutely passionate and know what you want to do. Identify your market. Be professional in your presentation and your business. Gardening is a vast area and there has got to be a bit where you fit. Identify that and go for it."

★ *www.gardenrescue.co.uk*

CASE STUDY

GILLY POLLOCK
BRITISH PLANT NURSERY GUIDE

Networker Gilly Pollock is the founder of the British Plant Nursery Guide, an organisation launched in 2010 to promote good quality, independent nurseries at shows, events and through its quintessentially British Plant Nursery Guide website (*www.britishplantnurseryguide.co.uk*). Here, plant enthusiasts (of which Gilly has a database of 5,000) can source local and specialist nurseries, check out any courses or events these nurseries have organised, and receive newsletter updates.

 Paid-up British Plant Nursery Guide members (of which there are 30 and counting) are all fantastic growers. Gilly insists they produce at least 50% of their own plants to be allowed to join and further have the evidence, including glasshouses and polytunnels, on-site for customers to see. Members include independent garden centres, one-man/woman outfits such as Damhead Nursery in Scotland (see Chapter 4) and some well-recognised names like the Duchy of Cornwall.

The British Plant Nursery Guide takes a stand at a number of garden shows, including the RHS Chelsea Flower Show (where gardeners can 'meet the grower') and Gardeners' World Live, plus smaller, regional events. These shows have enabled Gilly and her team to meet and develop a highly selective database and forge contacts with TV and newspaper gardening journalists with whom they keep in touch via email and phone.

"Because we visit our members and really get to know them, we can speak honestly about our nurseries at the shows," Gilly says. It was one such meeting that secured the British Plant Nursery Guide's regular Garden Notes slot in *Country Living*.

But Gilly's network extends far beyond the press, public and potential customers to friends of the guide, among them garden designers, paving and timber product companies, even a Morris Minor specialist which lends Morris Minor Travellers for the British Plant Nursery Guide's vintage-themed show stands. Further, Gilly has developed a relationship with charities such as Gardening Leave, which helps serving and ex-service personnel through horticultural therapy. "Partnerships like this are so beneficial for all parties and we meet many interesting people this way," Gilly explains.

She is an avid gardener, trained in horticulture, though her background is in HR. Her parents gardened too and it was from them she learnt "everything – digging, pruning, sowing seeds, dividing and understanding plant families and how to grow all sorts of plants". Her elderly father needed care in later life and, as Gilly sat looking after him, she decided it was time to change her life. "I'd never had that chance to reflect before and what I realised was that no one was representing these great nurseries," she says.

Gilly kept up her old job for the first two years, developing the new business in the evenings, at weekends and on days off. She "knocked on a few doors" in the early days when researching, including that of Jekka McVicar of Jekka's Herb Farm fame (*www.jekkasherbfarm.com*). "She was very nice and wished me luck, but I had no idea she was quite so well-known," Gilly says. She has since left her job (though plans to consult) to dedicate more time to the British Plant Nursery Guide. This she does with the help of husband Dave "who has been the sounding board and silent partner of the business" and, more recently, local consultant Katie Cripwell, who provides extra PR and marketing support.

Gilly thrives on meeting new people. She says: "Networking is so important to any business. While our nurseries are busy growing, I am on the look-out for new opportunities for them. Every day brings something new and it's about seizing the moment and sharing the benefits – it's very exciting." One thousand supporters have signed up to the British Plant Nursery Guide's current campaign, Flying the Flag for British Nurseries, pledging to cut plant miles and support local businesses by buying from local growers. A telecommunications company is using a member nursery to shoot its online ad campaign at the weekend and a series of British Plant Nursery Guide events in London, plus a book, are in the pipeline.

Gilly no longer has a day off but loves what she does. Her top tip is this:

"Remain true to your core values and your passion – without them you won't succeed."

★ *www.britishplantnurseryguide.co.uk*

CHAPTER 8

PR and Promotion

O f course, the best form of PR is a happy customer who will refer you and your services to their friends and help your business bloom. But as well as that, there are other tools in your box and you can't afford to ignore them. Let's take a look at them . . .

ONLINE

The internet has to be your second-most powerful networking and promotional tool (after word-of-mouth referrals).

Search engine optimisation

Firstly, using the web to promote your business means search engine optimisation (SEO) – i.e. making sure your website comes up on page one of a Google search for something relevant to your business.

This is achieved by clever manipulation of keywords and text (which you can pay an expert to do for you), generating links to other sites and updating your website regularly with new pictures of what your business is doing, including a blog if you have time.

If this is something you are keen to get to grips with yourself, here are some basic SEO principles:

* constantly look for other sites that can link back to you; make daily requests to build the numbers up, offering to add their link to your site if it makes sense (but *don't* target irrelevant or dubious sources)

* add good content, aimed at meeting a *need*: provide solutions; these get linked to and they get searched for

* ensure your page titles reflect the theme of the page and are a little promotional: they are what will appear in search results, and need to entice visitors to your site (don't go overboard, though)

* avoid repeating text that appears elsewhere on the web or your own site: duplicate text depresses your ranking, especially if the text appears on sites with a higher ranking than yours; if someone has reposted a lot of your material, ask them to withdraw it and provide a link instead

* don't leave text hidden on your site, or in the same or similar shade as the background; and don't stuff any page full of random keywords: search engines look for these as reasons to demote a site in their rankings.

Social networks

Secondly, online promotion means making use of social networks – Facebook, Twitter and LinkedIn – as Hunting Brook Gardens, The Traditional Flower Company, British Plant Nursery Guide and Coolings Nurseries all featured in this book have done.

Working with gardens lends itself really well to sharing online; your business will almost certainly provide you with a steady stream of beautiful photographs and interesting ideas to share. That's ideal for successful social networking, because the last thing you want to do is sign up and just shout at people about your business.

The key lies in being interesting, helpful and available rather than *directly* promoting.

★ Create a business page on Facebook (*www.facebook.com/page*), where customers can 'like' your business and any great content that you post. Upload videos and photos; offer advice. Respond to all feedback and questions. It's a terrific way to build a loyal following. You can also use Facebook to run time-limited offers on plants, garden tickets or project quotes; or take advantage of its paid-for advertising to target potential customers with great precision. Check out the free Enterprise Nation guide for more on successfully building your business on Facebook: *www.enterprise nation.com/facebook-book-offer*

★ Sign up for a Twitter account (*twitter.com/signup*), and use HootSuite (*www.hootsuite.com*) or TweetDeck (*www.tweet deck.com*) to schedule a steady stream of informative, amusing tweets: share your expertise, interesting photos, the quotes of happy customers, and engage with other businesses and industry influencers on the network.

★ Use LinkedIn (*www.linkedin.com*) to make connections with the big cheeses in your area who can help take your business to the next level. Fill up your network with satisfied customers, reliable suppliers, colleagues and friends. Then start looking for those who might be able to help you with a project or a client. LinkedIn lets you search by company, job title, location and industry, and then shows you how the people in the results are connected to your network. You might know the perfect person to make a fruitful introduction for you.

Video

Online videos on YouTube (*www.youtube.com*) or Vimeo (*www.vimeo.com*) can be a great way to demonstrate your know-how and let people see your beautiful past work. For a really good example, see expert tutorials posted by Bristol-based Posh Gardens owner Bob Latham on his website *www.poshgardens.com*.

It's best to keep videos under two minutes for maximum engagement (data shows rapid viewer drop-off after this). Be sure to use a good quality HD camera, and either replace the wind-blown microphone noises with a soundtrack or narration recorded *inside*!

iMovie is all you'll need for editing on Macs; and Adobe Premier Elements is good for PCs.

Contact database

Build a database. This will be especially useful for independent nursery owners who will be able to post or email updated plant lists to their customers throughout the year.

When Hannah Powell returned to help promote her family's business – Perrywood garden centre and nursery in Essex – after a ten-year stint working in PR and with business start-ups in London, she started out collecting names by getting customers to fill in comment cards in the store which were then entered into a prize draw. She created a database out of these names and others who signed up through Facebook and Twitter.

"It's good to have a list of loyal customers when we have something to promote," Hannah says. News and monthly updates are delivered directly to customers' inboxes, and in-store events and charity work are flagged up. "We want to be seen not just as another retailer on the high street, but as something customers can relate to," she says.

Try MailChimp (*mailchimp.com*), a useful program for managing your email marketing – from organising lists to sending out emails.

LOCAL PRESENCE

You'll also want to generate a local presence. Give talks at local plant societies and build a reputation as a plant expert in your area, organise nursery or open garden workshops to teach customers (for example) the basics of pruning, planting containers, seasonal maintenance or propagating techniques.

Have a sign with your logo and contact details outside the house where you are working.

If you are a designer or a garden coach, why not showcase your skills and open your garden to the public through the National Gardens Scheme as Louise Dowding in the next chapter does?

Coolings Nurseries chairman Paul Cooling says: "In the early days, going out and talking to WI and other groups, giving demonstrations on how to plant a hanging basket, all those things, can be hugely helpful in terms of building credibility and PR and it's something that, even after all these years, we still do."

WRITING

If you have a talent for writing, why not contribute a regular gardening feature to your village magazine or local newspaper? You could start a monthly gardening notes column, write a tried-and-tested garden products page, visit and write about nearby historic or open gardens, or put together a nursery owner's/garden designer's blog-style diary. It will do wonders for your profile and hopefully generate some extra income.

Getting press coverage

If the thought of writing articles fills you with dread but you have an interesting story to tell – such as a new nursery or an award-winning garden – then get in touch with your local newspaper or magazine features editor and let the experts take over.

How do you secure press coverage for your business? *Chichester Observer* chief reporter Lewis Brown explains that having a local angle is crucial to getting a story in print. "If it's national, there is nothing we can do with it," he says. He advises calling the news desk first, as emails are easily lost or overlooked, before sending across information. Attaching a photograph is also useful.

Avoid the day before publication as that is when newspaper staff will be at their busiest. And give as much notice as possible for feature ideas, which take some time to write. The resulting coverage will be a valuable, third-party endorsement that money can't buy.

"PR is about getting good news stories out there," says Hannah Powell of Perrywood garden centre and nursery. She cites the example of one member of staff who wore his shorts to work throughout the winter to raise money for Cancer Research. Hannah contacted local paper the *Essex Chronicle* who loved the story. Retail sales assistant Stuart Hancock appeared in print and raised £1,600 for a good cause.

NATIONAL PRESENCE

Down the line – and depending on your ambitions or type of business, perhaps not that far down the line – you'll need to think big and generate a national presence.

If you have a fantastic new gardening school to promote or have designed a high-end new garden that is now picture perfect, then get in touch with the gardening or features editor of the publication you think your story is most suited to.

You could also go direct to a freelance gardening writer or photographer whose work you have seen published (the Professional Garden Photographers' Association has a list of members on its site at *www.gpauk.org*), just as enterprising Georgia Miles, featured later in the chapter, did.

Fiona McLeod (*www.fionamcleod.com*) is The Plant Specialist nursery's gardening photographer of choice (see Chapter 10) and has work published in *The English Garden*, *Garden Design Journal* and *Gardens Illustrated* magazines.

"Gardening photographers are rarely commissioned," she explains. "So they take pictures first, and then find a publication that wants them."

This means Fiona is always looking for new things to take pictures of. Her advice on getting in print?

"Be aware that gardening magazines work a whole year in advance. So you must work out the best time of year for your garden or nursery to be photographed. This means if you have a garden opening in 2013, it would be worth getting pictures done now so it is publicised next year."

Advertising

Look at conventional paper advertising with caution: it can be pricey, and you ideally need a regular presence for at least 12 months for your investment to pay off.

Be absolutely certain its readership matches that of your target market before splashing out.

CASE STUDY
JAMES ALEXANDER-SINCLAIR
LANDSCAPE DESIGNER

Budding garden designers will be familiar with the name James Alexander-Sinclair. A successful and well-respected designer, his gardens appear regularly in newspapers and magazines. He is charming, funny and irreverent; a regular magazine contributor who blogs from his home Blackpitts in Northamptonshire as well as for *Gardener's World* magazine and online plant retailer Crocus. But for me, it is his presenting BBC2's *Small Town Gardens* back in 2003 (the series which prompted my own garden design studies) for which he is best known.

James started out 25 years ago as a landscape contractor because he "basically had nothing else to do. I was living at my sister's flat, lying on her sofa and smoking a lot of cigarettes. There was some frustration among my family and my sister said, 'Go and dig the garden!'"

He did, and found he rather liked and was good at it. He dug another and another and another until it became a business – Terra Firma Landscapes. In 1992, small children prompted a move from Camberwell, south-east London, to the greenery of rural Northamptonshire where James and his wife bought a derelict farmhouse. You can read all about the creation of their own beautiful one-acre plot there on James' website, *www.blackpitts.co.uk*.

And it was here, having already taken a ten-week course at the upmarket Inchbald School of Design eight years previously – he regrets not having taken his time over this and "done the Wisley or the Kew thing. I would have caught up so much quicker" – he decided to focus on garden design.

Business went well but a phone call request to design the garden for yet another vicarage – James describes this as Old Rectory Syndrome – prompted him to write a speculative article and send it off to a number of magazines, among them *Country Living* which commissioned his first gardening series. "I had to spread my wings," he says. A chance encounter with the editor of the *Daily Express* led to James designing an RHS Chelsea Flower Show garden for the newspaper in 1999, where he appeared on TV and so on . . .

"These things tend to fall in place. There was some luck involved and, I would also like to think, it is something I am good at," he says.

In the meantime, his garden design business continued to grow. Today his work breaks down into a 70/30 garden design/media split. His work is on predominantly large, country acreages, photos of which can be found on his website. He works with clients for an average of ten years, building gardens a bit at a time. "Gardening is what I do," explains James. "Most of my income comes from this and it's what I love."

Much work comes through recommendation, some through location (one client told James, "I have looked at Dan Pearson, Cleve West and Tom Stuart Smith and you are the closest"), and some from print coverage "especially in the *FT*", James says. "But usually such articles just add another layer to one's profile, helpful, but often not translatable into concrete business."

James is a busy man, so much so that the interview to write this piece was conducted on the phone in a 30-minute slot, James en route to a client appointment. He had given a series of lectures at the Gardener's World Live show in Birmingham at the weekend, been filming with Cleve West and Joe Swift the previous day (check out *Three Men Went to Mow* on YouTube) and was off to the Gardeners' Fair at historic house Cottesbrooke Hall to give lectures and run a mini design studio at the weekend.

"I'm very lucky that I enjoy what I do. I wake up happy in the mornings. But this also means I work long days. We are not rich but no one has starved, we have not ended up homeless and I have never missed one of my children's sports days or school concerts. It is enormous freedom but it comes at a price."

James' top tip is this:

"Look after your clients as no amount of press coverage or snazzy leaflets will be nearly as effective as a good recommendation. The best advertising is passed between friends."

CASE STUDY
Georgia Miles
The Sussex Flower School

In a large, weather-boarded studio down a quiet country lane in the East Sussex village of Laughton, six women are learning to hand-tie a bouquet of flowers. Their tutor, Georgia Miles, is a former English teacher turned floristry lecturer. She decided that, though the market for short, luxury horticultural courses was well catered for, what was missing were affordable (£95 a day), technical, up-skilling days. "I wanted to plug all gaps in the market, to offer something to people for whom, for whatever reason – be that family or work commitments – going back to college was not an option," she explains.

Georgia is a keen gardener and her own beautiful, three quarter-acre plot, complete with its own cutting garden, is the source of inspiration for the school. Classes are predominantly flower-based, though simple garden design, willow-weaving and cake decorating are also available, as are children's parties, art classes, even wild mushroom foraging. Each week, customers come from London, Surrey, Sussex and Kent, others from as far as Scotland and the south-west of England to learn how to design a table display, arrange wedding flowers or tackle a difficult border. "We give them proper coffee, a lovely lunch and send them away at the end of the day with confidence," Georgia says.

Launching the business was a leap of faith, "Though not a blind leap of faith. I had done quite a lot of research. I knew there was a gap in the market and was confident of my expertise," Georgia says. She called in the experts at the outset, commissioning design agency Judd Associates to develop branding that would run throughout the website, stationery and other promotional material. The £1,500 invested in this, she says, was money well spent.

The name, The Sussex Flower School, means her school is readily found on Google and other search engine sites, and her website's slick, professional look means customers are happy to make bookings online. Georgia promotes her school at The Garden Show at Stanstead Park in Hampshire, where she and I met, and at shows at Firle Place and Loseley Park. "They are cost-effective, good for business and great fun," she says. "I always run a competition and have something inexpensive but lovely for sale on the stand."

She also had some "really beautiful" A5 cards printed which she "leaves everywhere" – in shops, hairdressers and pinned to village noticeboards. "The cards have proved very successful," Georgia says, as has advertising her school in local magazine *Wealden Times*. "It is good because the readership is exactly my area and it is perceived as quality, though you can pick it up for free. It often turns up in doctors' surgeries months later, so I made sure all advertising is non-date specific," she says. Georgia has also contacted other websites and gardening bloggers, such as From Britain with Love (*www.frombritainwithlove.com*) and Flowerona (*flowerona.com*), and uses Twitter to tweet about her school. "I network constantly without being too pushy – there is nothing worse," she says.

Her proactive take on PR led her to contact gardening photographer Suzie Gibbons (*www.flowerpowerpictures.com*) and, in turn, to her first magazine article – a two-page piece in a country lifestyle magazine.

"I saw Suzie had taken photos of a company similar to mine, so I emailed her to ask her how she worked," says Georgia. "She came and took photos, sold them to a magazine and then their writer contacted me for the actual words. It didn't cost me a thing."

Since then another photographer who found Georgia through her website has been in touch for a Christmas shoot for local glossy *Sussex Life*.

Business is going well at The Sussex Flower School. So much so that Georgia has just relocated from her home studio in the garden to a new, rented space up the road. This means more room and that her house and garden which, for the last two years have been an extension of The Sussex Flower School brand, no longer have to look immaculate at all times – tricky when you are juggling running a business with looking after three children aged 10 to 13.

Georgia's top tip is this:

"Don't start until you have sorted out your brand because once that image is out there, you don't want to be changing it too much."

★ *www.thesussexflowerschool.co.uk*

CHAPTER 9

Dealing with Customers

The customer is all-important. However well-trained and well-organised you are, and no matter how well you have promoted yourself and your new venture, without customers you have no business.

So spend some time thinking about your customer service, and make sure any staff you have working with you are onside.

Presentation

Being likeable and presentable will go a long way towards getting the commission or making the sale. How charming you are, how professional you and your premises look will determine the kind of service your customers expect – and whether they will be prepared to spend money with you or not.

This means having the right kit and clothing for the job, being well-prepared for client meetings, driving a clean van, keeping your nursery tidy and weed-free and knowing your plants.

"Appearance makes a huge difference," says Paul Cooling of Coolings Nurseries. His staff are uniformed, wear a name badge and carry a walkabout phone so back-up is never far away. And if the nursery gets busy, Paul goes onto the shopfloor himself to help out.

"We take great pride in the fact that there aren't weeds or disease in our plants for sale. It gives customers confidence this is the right place to come."

Repeat custom

If a client or customer is delighted with the service you provide, they will hopefully keep coming back. Paul says this can often mean thinking for them, even if it means losing the sale – pointing out, for example, that the fast-growing tree they have chosen for their garden will quickly block the view from their kitchen window and so perhaps a slower-growing variety, even if it's not one that Coolings Nurseries stocks, would be more suitable.

"You might lose the sale in the short term, but the customer will go away thinking you have been helpful and come back. This has been proven time and again," he says.

Manage expectations

Prepare your client for the fact that real-life gardens are not like the ones you see on TV and that plants and planting schemes take time to mature – up to three years for borders and six for hedges, though planting fast-growing perennials and installing an irrigation system can really help speed things up.

Explain how long a project is going to take and warn clients it can be a messy business in the meantime. Pick up your mobile when it rings, and keep clients updated and informed via phone or email, especially if the schedule starts to slide . . .

Garden designer Moira Farnham explains:

"When a garden is being built, there is great theatre at the outset when the client comes home from work and their old garden has gone. But then when the hard landscaping starts and the pace begins to slow, the perception can be that work has gone off the boil."

Flagging this process up is important, as is preparing customers for how long plants take to get established. "The less of a gardener and the more of a lifestyler they are, the more difficult this can be," she says.

Being the expert

Be firm. You are the trained professional and, while the client will have ideas as to what they want, ultimately it is down to you to deliver their vision, and it is you, the expert, who will know whether the client's choice of plant, ideas on garden features, or indeed the budget they have for a project, will work. Landscape designer James Alexander-Sinclair says:

> "The client relationship is so important. I am very bossy and tell clients what to do. They may be good at hedge-funding but that doesn't mean they know where to plant one."

This also means telling customers how to look after the plants you recommend or have sold them. Consider providing written instructions; Architectural Plants sends its shoppers home with these, and its online catalogue has a red, amber, green system to denote plant hardiness.

Know your value

Don't be apologetic for charging (provided your fees are in line with the competition, of course). Materials, plants and labour come at a cost, as does your time as a trained professional who knows what plants will work where.

"In the early days I probably did more physical work than I wanted. I didn't get the pricing right and sold myself short," says Pod Garden Design's Mark Yabsley. It takes time to develop confidence and realise your worth but he recommends you counter the charge: "That's expensive," with: "Compared to what?"

Professionalism

Be considerate and professional. Leave sites safe, clean and tidy. Sweep up and don't tread muddy boots through a client's house. Keeping the client onside is crucial.

"That means everything from closing the gates so their dog doesn't escape, to not blocking their car when they need to get out for the school run, not leaving cigarette butts lying around in the garden and not having the radio on loudly," says Moira Farnham. "These things matter on a project that can last two or three months or even more. If a landscape contractor is getting in the clients' hair at the end of week one, imagine what it will be like by weeks four and five."

Keep a bit of a distance (see the advice of Louise Dowding later in the chapter). These are your clients, not your friends. Should something go wrong – should the client not like the choice of stone-paving, the location of a tree or if newly-laid turf fails – it is easier to deal with if you have maintained a professional working relationship. Deal with complaints politely and promptly, and don't avoid the situation. It will only make matters worse.

Learn to say no

And finally, in the nicest possible way, learn to say 'no thank you' to difficult jobs that might break your tools or damage your back. Turn down work you don't really want for clients you don't much like.

Gardener Gary Edwards' advice is this: "Avoid bad customers, especially in a small place where everyone knows everyone else." Anyone who has been through two or more gardeners in the last year, for example.

"If there is trouble, just walk away as nicely as possible. When you first start out you want all business," he says. "But as you build up, you can cherry pick your jobs."

Designer Denise Cadwallader agrees:

"Go and see the client, take a portfolio – these days it's generally on an iPad – take a brief and a good look at the garden. But don't offer hundreds of ideas. And never do any work without a signed contract. If you ever get an adverse feeling, the likelihood is you are not going to get on and you need to say: 'This is not for me,' no matter how desperate you are."

CASE STUDY
LOUISE DOWDING
DESIGNER AND GARDENER

From the road there is no inkling of what lies on the other side of Louise and Fergus Dowding's Somerset farmhouse. Walk through the hall and the windows frame a sea of plants at shoulder height, beckoning you outside. Abundantly planted rectangular borders face square vegetable beds surrounded by box hedging and espaliered apple trees. Louise is a garden designer and here has achieved the gardener's Holy Grail of year-round interest.

She trained first as a sculptor and then as a landscape architect before leaving London for Somerset and a life in the country. Once in the West Country, Louise embarked on a one-year garden design course at Kingston Maurwood College in Dorset, before working as an assistant to the well-known garden writer and designer Penelope Hobhouse. "You can do as many courses as you like but they won't teach you about plants – what they do, how they die and how badly behaved they can be," Louise says.

Her own beautiful, one-acre plot, which opens once a year to the public or gardening groups by appointment for the National Gardens Scheme, serves as a useful showroom. Here clients can take a look and see what they love and would like replicated in their own gardens, and more importantly, says Louise, what they don't want. The garden has been widely featured in newspapers and gardening magazines. While this kind of press coverage hasn't ever actually generated a new job, says Louise, it does help reinforce a client's decision to go ahead and use her. "If I'm in print it means I'm probably OK," she says.

Family commitments mean her business is local, within a 30 to 40-mile radius of home. Typical clients are well-off, who have "sold well" in London and moved to a rambling, country house with a ten to 15-acre garden, perhaps untouched since the 1970s and with the same gardener for the last 40 years. Therefore Louise is dependent not just on developing a good relationship with the client, but also on winning the trust of the client's gardener who will be responsible for maintaining and developing her vision once the project is finished. "It's difficult. You are tearing up a garden they have worked on all that time and expecting them to support you in this," she says.

The process works like this. A client rings up explaining she would like the family garden designed. Louise suggests a few possibilities and states her hourly rate and travel charge, confirming this in writing. All being well, Louise makes a site visit and discusses with the client what the client would like. (They generally have quite clear ideas and have been collecting magazine articles as inspiration.) Louise then instructs a surveyor to do a plan of the site and, from this, develops a master plan which marries the client's ideas with her own. "Sometimes this process is quick and sometimes it is a struggle," Louise says.

"You'll like someone or not more or less straightaway," she says, "but that doesn't necessarily reflect how well you will work with them. You are putting people under a huge amount of stress by bulldozing their garden, and you never know quite how they will react."

She typically takes on four or five new projects each year which are built over the summer and then planted in the following spring. Once the garden is completed – and Louise doesn't get involved with the building side at all – she places the plants for planting, again, by someone else.

The client relationship continues if they then want their garden managed or if, as many do at a later stage, they decide to extend the newly planted formal gardens surrounding the house into wild flower meadows, orchards, woodland walks and ponds. Louise makes sure she keeps a cool, professional distance throughout.

"I want my clients to be able to speak their minds and, if a friendship develops then I am delighted, but that is later, after the project has finished, and is at their instigation."

What if something goes wrong and the client does have to speak their mind? "I panic at night," says Louise, "and then go and face it the next day."

Her advice to anyone looking to set up their own gardening business is to "be absolutely passionate about what you do. Otherwise it's completely pointless. You can see it in a garden if someone is interested or not. And, if they are not, it lacks that buzz, that excitement, that vision," she says.

★ *www.louisedowding.co.uk*

CASE STUDY
ALISON MARSDEN
GARDENING BY DESIGN

Alison Marsden describes herself as a knowledgeable lady gardener. She offers a garden-coaching service for people who want to improve or create their own gardens without the help of a designer, but who don't know how. She also teaches gardening courses for Kent Adult Education Services and gives gardening talks at Riverhill Himalayan Gardens in Sevenoaks (featured on TV's *Country House Rescue*). The success of her business depends on getting on well with her clients and being a good speaker. "I have always enjoyed sharing knowledge and finding different ways of explaining things to people," she says.

Like so many others profiled in this book, gardening is Alison's second career. Her first was in software management. She now interweaves the two, having moved out of full-time employment into part-time consultancy. "I really loved my first career but love gardening too, and now I use many of the same problem-solving and communication skills in both," she explains.

Alison grew up in the country and in her early 20s got involved in voluntary conservation work, such as coppicing and clearing ponds. Her future husband, Richard, did too and, once married, they moved out of London to Kent and their own garden. Here

Alison "got hooked" on gardening, read up and took her RHS General Certificate followed by a garden design correspondence course.

One evening, as Alison and Richard sat watching a TV gardening show, he said to her: "Stop talking back at the programme. Just be quiet, or do something about it." At that point, it occurred to Alison that what people *really* needed was not necessarily a garden designer but the knowledge and understanding to develop their own gardens themselves, and that what she should become was a gardening coach.

Except no such thing seemed to exist back in 2004 when she started out. Unsure what her new label should be, she settled on Gardening by Design – i.e. gardening by design not by accident. Her technology background meant she was happy to build her own website and so she set out slowly establishing her business, with a little advertising, some local newspaper PR and word-of-mouth referrals.

Her customers are predominantly owners of small gardens and include first-time home-owners, parents wanting to create family-friendly spaces and the actively retired who want to get into gardening. "It comes to us all in the end, it's just a matter of when," Alison smiles. Some are total beginners, others want advice on garden layout but choose their own plants.

"But just as not everyone wants a unique architect-designed house, not every family wants a cutting-edge garden," she explains. "What they want is a place to eat, somewhere for children to play and plenty of year-round interest to complement their house."

The process works like this. The client gets in touch in need of help and Alison goes to see them in their own garden. She looks, listens, discusses what they have, what they want, styles they do and don't like and how much time they want to spend gardening.

She explains soil type, orientation and surroundings to help decide what stays, what gets moved and what ends up as compost. Typical consultations last an hour to an hour-and-a-half. Alison can also conduct simple site surveys and provide a basic outline plan and written report if requested.

"While people will happily rip out curtains and carpets they don't like in a new house, they are often afraid to do the same in their gardens," explains Alison. "But a little bit of knowledge gives a lot of confidence to make changes. They say: 'Now you have explained I understand.'"

Alison is awaiting the results of her second set of RHS Level 3 exams as we speak and, though customers are not interested in details of her qualifications, they are impressed by her ability to identify plants (especially when not flowering), to explain growing cycles and the impact of different soil types – why friends in the neighbouring village can grow rhododendrons, for example, and they can't. "I could not, hand on heart, stand up and teach something I didn't understand at a deeper level. And if there is something I can't identify, I say so, take a picture and get back to them," she says.

The fact that it takes time to put Alison's advice into practice means repeat business is slow. "It's a flawed business model in that sense," she says, "but the reward is in seeing families create their own great gardens". She cites the example of one customer who called back after two years and said: "Come and see what I have done." "It was lovely," Alison says. "A conservatory and a patio had been built, the lawn was reshaped and he was ready to talk about the detailed planting."

Her advice to anyone looking to set up their own gardening business is: "Be clear about what you want to offer and who your customers are and then go for it."

★ *www.gardeningbydesign.co.uk*

CHAPTER 10

Developing Your Business

So your business has been up and running for some time now, and doing well. While your original plan will have set a framework for development, it is likely that your new venture will have taken on a life of its own, determined by the market, what your customers want, what you find you are best at, what makes you most money and what you most enjoy.

When I lived in London and was running my own landscape-design company, for example, my business partner and I found that, though being out on-site, meeting clients and designing garden master plans was the most enjoyable part of the job, it was through the mark-up made on plants supplied that we made most money. That, and writing. So we concentrated much of our effort on offering a soft landscaping and planting service, while factoring my writing time into our weekly schedule.

"Most businesses start with a plan and objectives, but you have to be ready to grab new opportunities," says Hannah Powell of Perrywood garden centre and nursery. "I haven't met many entrepreneurs and start-ups who are where they planned to be five years ago. Some ideas fly. Others don't."

Growing your gardening business could mean some of the following . . .

Increasing sales

Increasing sales is a direct way of growing your business. It depends, of course, on your capacity for taking on the extra work. Mike Kitchen of Rocket Gardens, profiled later in this chapter, took this route in dramatic style. His greenhouse enterprise started just seven years ago and has grown to the point that it dispatches an amazing two million plants UK-wide each year.

When increasing sales you should be able to get advice and support from the relevant organisations listed in Chapter 4, though do be aware that the bigger your business becomes, the more time you will spend actually *running* it, as opposed to being outside doing the thing that you love . . .

Taking on staff

Perhaps the time has come to take on a knowledgeable full- or part-time assistant to look after your plants, undertake manual gardening work, help with the design process by putting your sketched ideas onto computer, organise the office or deal with customer orders.

With staff come new responsibilities – contracts, paying a salary other than your own, health and safety, insurance, running a payroll, holiday and sick pay, all of which your accountant and/or business support organisation can advise on. You can also go to the *www.gov.uk* website to find out more.

"When you are small it is relatively easy to keep control over your business," Perrywood's Hannah Powell says. "Once you have ten, 20 or even 30 staff, you have to let go and let others help you to develop your vision. Not everyone wants to go that way. It's a personal choice and it depends on what you want out of life."

Expanding your premises

Growing your gardening business could mean investing in new premises to separate your home and work life (thus freeing up your garage and driveway from plant deliveries, vans, mowers and tools), or expanding the site you already have. You could grow a wider range of plants, make way for a new garden building for lectures or talks, or find a place for add-ons such as garden sculptures and pots.

Georgia Miles, who we met back in Chapter 8, says: "It was really good to run the business from home for the first two years and not to have to pay any rent. It gave me the courage to get started, but I think it is easy to get to a certain stage and then rest on your laurels. I am ready for the next challenge now, to be forced to earn more."

New products or services

You could launch new products and services, as the majority of businesses profiled in this book have done. You could add garden repairs or a terrace-planting service to your offerings, or hire out potted topiary for weddings and events. You could offer maintenance, do garden coaching, write features on plants.

Award-winning Coolings Nurseries in Kent has two garden centres (the second opened in 2004). These sell homegrown plants, plus garden-related gifts, BBQs and garden furniture, with a coffee shop at each site. The nursery runs courses, is an RHS-approved training provider (which means you can study for your RHS Level 2 Principles of Horticulture here) and hosts talks and events. Further, it offers tree-planting and garden coaching, with a new autumn 'garden to bed' and spring 'wake-up' service for clients, for which it has recruited two maintenance gardeners who are kept busy all year round. "Our growth has been a gradual evolution based on what people like, what they dislike, what our competitors are doing and what is working for them, and responding to those trends," chairman Paul Cooling says.

Better equipment

Growing your gardening business could mean investing some of the money you have made into buying new equipment which will help you do your job faster, more efficiently or professionally. This might include computer software, a second van with your logo on the side, new tools, a more comprehensive website or printed promotional material for point-of-sale.

Longer opening hours

Maybe you will decide to extend your garden or nursery opening times to a regular Monday to Saturday 9am to 5pm throughout the year. Perhaps you are ready to give up your old job and devote yourself to your new venture full-time. Maybe your hours have been restricted by childcare since your little ones came along and, once they start school, you can increase your time spent designing, teaching or coaching.

Entering awards

You could raise your profile by entering (and ideally winning) local or national trade body awards, or an RHS medal at one of its Flower Shows. You could gain full membership to the organisation of your choice. Landscape designer Jonnie Wake explains:

> "Many potential clients looking for a garden builder, gardener or designer will look here first. It is a stamp of approval from the industry itself."

The Society of Garden Designers passes on details of its full accredited members to researchers and journalists looking for ideas and stories, which means they are the ones you get to see in magazines and on television.

Be the go-to expert

You could make a name as an expert in your field, be that for specialist pruning, selling cottage-style perennials, designing contemporary gardens, planting living willow hedging or clipping shapes out of box. Writing, giving demonstrations or talks, even being interviewed on the radio, all these things would help underline this expertise (and hopefully allow you to raise prices).

Become more efficient

And finally, become more efficient by looking for more profitable work – be that public-speaking, taking on lawn-mowing and hedge-trimming which pays well but is relatively quick and easy to do, or looking for lucrative commercial contracts.

Gardeners Guild founder Gary Edwards explains: "We try to encourage our members to think of growing their businesses not in terms of increasing prices or working longer hours, but in terms of planning ahead." This might mean starting up a paid-for garden waste collection service for customers which can be incorporated into your daily gardening round (and effectively means you get paid for making your daily trip to the tip). It might mean adding lawn treatment to your list of services for existing customers. It might mean selling pots and plants. The key is to think strategically so as to maximise what you can get paid for a day's work.

CASE STUDY
Sean Walter and Keith Pounder
The Plant Specialist

Turn right off the high street in Great Missenden, Bucks, over a railway bridge and there, on a four-acre patch opposite Gipsy House, the home and garden of late children's author Roald Dahl, is The Plant Specialist. It is part upmarket landscape design and build company, part grounds-maintenance contractor and part nursery specialising in ornamental grasses and herbaceous perennials. Here are ordered rows of verbena, hemerocallis, agapanthus and more unexpected finds. Colourful achillea bob about in the breeze. It is pure plant-lovers' heaven.

The company is run by fellow gardeners Sean Walter and Keith Pounder, who met working at Gipsy House. Keith had been head gardener there since 1989 and Sean – an expert plantsman working as a nursery plant buyer at the time and freelancing in his days off – was brought in to renovate the existing herbaceous borders. The pair hit it off and plans for The Plant Specialist were formed.

Their shared vision was for a specialist nursery offering unusual and interesting plants in a beautiful setting. "The challenge was how could we be a specialist nursery but have some kind of commercial savvy?" says Sean.

"All too often specialist nurseries are husband-and-wife teams selling at plant fares and in back yards, which is fantastic for customers who know what they are looking for, but isn't very inspiring if you don't know the first thing about plants."

However, without working capital "short of selling our houses", they launched a landscaping business in 1998 to earn the money to open the nursery and realise their dream.

Their early landscaping work was a marriage of Sean's existing freelance clients and Keith's local contacts. The business took off, expanded into garden, grounds and sports ground maintenance, and recruited its first four staff members as apprentices. "It is difficult to find qualified staff," says Sean, "so it's often easier to train them on the job."

Today, The Plant Specialist has up to two teams building gardens at any one time (plus a network of self-employed joiners, metal workers, a draftsman and even a garden photographer they can call on). "Our company growth has been an organic process," says Sean. "We have only employed new people when we realised we couldn't manage with what we had." Work quietens down in the winter, so recruiting just the right number is, says Sean, a fine balancing act. Similarly The Plant Specialist has only invested in new equipment, including vans, tractors, toppers and rotovators when it has had the money to do so.

Sean and Keith's long-awaited retail nursery opened in 2002 and employs a further six part-time staff, and supplies a small percentage of plants needed for client gardens – clearly there is scope for growth here. Making a profit out of plant sales, however, is something they are yet to achieve; stiff competition from cut-price multiples makes it difficult to raise prices. However, Sean and Keith plan to expand their nursery over the next two years (they currently only make use of half their four-acre site) and increase footfall, getting the nursery to a size where they can offer the full range they would like. The Plant Specialist website has been updated to this end, with an online plant catalogue. Online sales are set to follow, and the nursery display area is to be made more user-friendly, divided into areas for shade, dry shade, half-hardy plants, those that need full sun, grasses, etc.

Once this is in place, and Sean estimates the process will take a couple of years, the plan is to take stands at RHS shows and for a PR push (Sean has the RHS's *The Garden* magazine in mind).

"Editorial really is the best publicity you can get," he says. "We had a mention by Val Bourne in *The Telegraph* a few years ago and even now get people walking in with the article in their hands."

Their advice to anyone starting out now is: "Don't go in with preconceived ideas of what you are prepared to do. If you want to be a designer, be prepared to prune trees or plant up pots. Don't be too precious to do the small work, and do it well. And let your business grow out of that."

★ *www.theplantspecialist.co.uk*

CASE STUDY
MIKE KITCHEN
ROCKET GARDENS

Mike Kitchen is a man on a mission to get us growing our own food, whether we have half an acre to spare or space for just a few flowerpots. His business, Rocket Gardens, aims to make cultivating organic vegetables as easy as possible by germinating the seeds, growing them into healthy young plants and then dispatching them to home gardeners around the country.

Mike grew up in Cornwall and, when he returned, wanted to set up an environmentally-friendly business. "I had taken a year off work and spent the time growing vegetables. I realised the whole process was so time-consuming that only people who were retired would be able to do it," he explains.

The company started out on a rented, three-acre site. Early Rocket Gardens were grown here inside beautiful, if somewhat dilapidated, 1920s greenhouses belonging to a flower grower friend. "They were very photogenic, but leaky, impractical and difficult to maintain," says Mike. And prone to letting the biological pest control – the lacewings and ladybirds used to keep aphids under control – escape.

So three years ago, Rocket Gardens upped sticks and moved 15 miles down the road, to a 120-acre farm, most of which is used for cultivating spring greens, potatoes, rosemary and grassland (Mike trained in farm and estate management) with four acres dedicated to growing organic veg. A former herb farm, it came conveniently purpose-made, complete with a rainwater-recycling system and 23 large polytunnels. "It is huge in comparison to the old site but great for company growth," he says.

Business has expanded to such an extent that, this spring, Rocket Gardens shipped an astonishing two million plants UK-wide – a number that is growing all the time.

"I plan to help lots more people enjoy growing their own," says Mike. "We currently help more than 1,000 schools grow their own vegetables and we'd like to encourage children to teach their parents."

Much is couriered up to London, some as far north as Scotland and northern England. The whole process, from growing to packaging to shipping, is overseen by Mike who has recruited staff to man the operations, namely a nursery manager, four-strong office team and a casual, seasonal workforce of up to 20 when needed.

The company has a strict eco policy. Everything is grown organically without artificial heat. Customer plant orders are sent out in recycled cardboard boxes snugly packed around with straw for shipping. The idea, Mike explains, is that everything in the box should be biodegradable.

"West Cornwall is ahead of the season anyway and we can grow a month before most places, even two, without using heat. If you are growing organically, you should try not to use fossil fuel to do it. If the fuel going into growing your crops is greater than what's coming out in terms of food values, there's an imbalance."

Mike has seen "a definite shift in the way people think about food and we have tried to follow the trend for seasonal produce". While he and his team started out selling instant vegetable gardens, this has since expanded into fruit and herbs, as well as spring/summer and autumn/winter gardens. The majority of Rocket Gardens' sales are made online and these days its products are in demand year-round, with rocket, beans, beetroot and cauliflower going out in the spring, followed by kale, cabbages, spinach and chard going out in the autumn. Christmas gifts keep Rocket Gardens busy right through what would otherwise be quiet winter months.

Mike's latest venture is a Constant Gardens package – a year-round supply of plants delivered throughout the year ensuring a continual supply of home grown organic vegetables. Included in the price is one week's free camping at Rockets' newly-opened campsite. Here, holiday makers can pitch up, enjoy the countryside and get an insight into how Rocket gardens are grown.

Mike's top tip?

"There are lots of opportunities to develop your business out there, but you need to be clear in your mind that you are focusing on the right one. And you have to see things through," he says. "I find I have loads and loads of new ideas and not enough time to get them all finished."

★ *www.rocketgardens.co.uk*

CONCLUSION

Words from the Wise

I n the course of researching and writing this book, some valuable points came up over and over again. These were:

1. There is no shortage of work out there even in these finance-stricken times for reliable people who can do a good job.

2. Cost has become an important factor – look around for the best quote; make sure your client/customer is getting a good deal.

3. There's not enough plant knowledge out there. Too many designers, but not enough plants people.

4. So it's really important to get proper horticultural training.

5. Running your own gardening business is really tough work, especially at the start. It can take time to get going and get referrals.

6. Your early work will probably come through family and friends.

7. Ultimately word of mouth will become your most powerful marketing tool.

8. Finding a niche is key, as is building a sound network of contacts and a database of clients.

9. Never, ever work for someone you don't like.

10. Finally, you have to be absolutely passionate about what you do.

I also put the question, "What is the most important lesson you have learnt in running your own gardening business?" to the people profiled in this book and those who contributed in other ways.

And this is what they said . . .

ON STARTING OUT

Caroline De Lane Lea and Louise Cummins, Gardenmakers: "If we were starting again, we would invest more time and money in researching who our target market was to be, what kind of gardens we wanted to build and pitching ourselves accordingly; building up a portfolio of the Right Sort of Projects, if you like. We wish we had started with the end in mind."

"Do your research, spend time planning and get good advice from people you can trust."

Gilly Pollock, British Plant Nursery Guide: "Be patient and don't take too much notice of people who say 'But you're only small'. Don't give up – Rome wasn't built in a day. Successful businesses sometimes forget how it was when they started up. The most important thing is to do your research, spend time planning and get good advice from people you can trust. When the foundations are in place you can start building on them."

Mike Kitchen, Rocket Gardens: "I think you've got to be quite focused on making sure you can sell what you grow. You can grow all you like but if you haven't got a market it doesn't make much sense."

Sam Ellson, The Traditional Flower Company: "It is important to identify a niche product or service in the marketplace that will make your company stand out from your competitors and to get as close to your customer as possible, to test your product offer or service. The customer is king/queen so *listen* to the feedback and make sure you are flexible enough to change your business model. We thought we would target mainly online sales with a few weddings a year; now we are mainly weddings."

ON ORGANISATION

Angus White, Architectural Plants: "Despite resisting it with every fibre of my being, I have come to accept that you have to tow a few lines: have proper structure, staff contracts, etc. I hate it but it really is necessary."

Georgia Miles, The Sussex Flower School: "Be very, very organised with your paperwork from the beginning. Get a good accountant, one who does a good job and doesn't rip you off. I have a big file I put everything into and then hand it over. Believe in what you are doing and enjoy it. But make sure you stop sometimes. Women, especially mothers, are often pulled in lots of directions."

Juliet Sargeant, garden designer: "Garden designers are generally not good at business. If you find that you are like the rest of us in that, then either make an effort to develop the skills to earn your living doing what you love, or find someone who can help you."

Sue Gray, Damhead Nursery: "I would say it is important to try to develop a scaleable business model that works for a small start-up company and can be scaled up as your business develops."

ON CUSTOMER CARE

Caroline Knight, The Quiet Gardener: "Relationships are vital. Nobody will hire you for a second time or on a regular basis if you are unfriendly, inconsiderate or if you leave them with problems. However, clients need training. Ideally you should be able to let them know when to expect you – but they should also understand that the weather is an important factor and schedules can change because of this. Endeavour not to be treated like a member of the family. This is a professional relationship and you could easily waste a quarter of your earning power over coffee and walnut cake."

Gill Chamberlain, Garden Rescue: "Do business with people the way you would like people to do business with you. Realise that there are some people with whom you just don't have and cannot develop empathy, and so you can never work effectively for them. Learn to recognise them and pass them on to someone who can. Remember that you don't have to like a garden for it to be a success, people have very different tastes and, if the plants are healthy and performing and the client is happy, then you have achieved what you set out to do."

Graham Gough, Marchants Hardy Plants: "The public is much brighter than people give them credit for at times. So the lesson I have learnt is not to pre-judge them. In addition, try and set the highest possible standards it is physically possible to achieve."

James Alexander-Sinclair, landscape designer: "I never work for anyone I don't like. Because if I don't like them, the chances are they won't like me, won't like what I do and won't pay my bill. I go and see the client, spend a couple of hours there and at that point you know if there is a connection. If there isn't, I say, 'I don't think this is going to work. I'm too busy. Try someone else.' When you first start out, saying: 'I don't want this, thank you, goodbye,' is difficult to do. But it is the most important piece of advice I can ever give."

Louise Dowding, garden designer: "Listen to and understand your client. The gardener, who will maintain the garden long after the designer has gone, is king and will make or break your design."

"The gardener, who will maintain the garden long after the designer has gone, will make or break your design."

Sean Walter, The Plant Specialist: "You have to have absolute honesty with your client as you could be working with them for years. You have to be frank and direct with people. Don't tell them what they want to hear. And have the courage to walk away."

ON STAFF

Hannah Powell, Perrywood garden centre and nurseries: "Listen to advice from others but choose your own path and decide which advice fits your own vision for the business. If you listen to absolutely everyone you could end up losing your identity. It's OK to make mistakes as long as you learn from them. And, when you find a good member of staff who you can rely on to deliver your vision, hold onto them. They will be worth their weight in gold."

"Our staff turnover is low because we look after them and pay them well."

James Gubb, Streetscape: "You've got to make sure you go into business with people you work well with and respect. Focus on quality and delivering the highest standards not just in terms of the work you do, but also in how you relate to your staff and present yourself."

Paul Cooling, Coolings Nurseries: "The most important thing I have learned is to look after our people. Our staff turnover is low because we look after them and pay them well, and we make sure the right people are in the right jobs."

ON ATTITUDE

Alison Marsden, Gardening by Design: "The most important thing I have learned? This job doesn't come quickly or easily but it is hugely rewarding."

Denise Cadwallader, Garden Arts: "You've got to be a self-starter. I have lot of students who want to be spoon-fed. You've got to be very motivated and hardworking and prepared to get out there and find information for yourself."

Jimi Blake, Hunting Brook Gardens: "It's so important to keep the business evolving and moving forward. Feel the excitement of new ideas. Trust in your vision. People will keep coming to a garden that changes and offers something new each year."

Lisa Rawley, Fleur de Lys: "Keep doing what you enjoy the most; focus on the parts of the work that inspire you. This keeps you fresh and innovative. Find other people to join you and to take on the parts of the business you least enjoy."

Sarah Mead, Yeo Valley's Organic Garden: "If you are enthusiastic and welcoming, people will enjoy themselves – it's infectious. And always try to exceed people's expectations. We all love to get an unexpected bonus. We never charge for coffee *and* biscuits, we charge for coffee – and the biscuits are free."

Moira Farnham, Garden Design School: "Believe in yourself but without arrogance, and try to tread lightly on the Earth. By that I mean work harmoniously with the land, the site and the client. I want people to love their garden and to find it beautiful, of course, but mostly I want to get to a place where the garden feels *inevitable*, that it just has to be this way."

ON MANAGING PROJECTS

Hugo Bugg, garden designer: "Always use recommended contractors, subcontractors and so on, because there are loads of cowboys out there."

Jonnie Wake, Landmark Gardens: "Attention to detail is vital. As a *designer*, it's the detail within a scheme that gives a garden its charm and strength of character. Developing each element within a scheme will ensure your designs remain innovative and, in turn, will prevent you from developing habitual design patterns. As a *contractor*, a meticulous attention to detail during the construction phase will not only provide the appearance and longevity a client pays for, but will also save on unnecessary snagging costs. And as a *project manager*, attention to detail during the planning and site-works stages will at the very least offer you the illusion that you are in control. It will also enable you to keep abreast of costs and timing for everyone's benefit."

ON FINANCES

Gary Edwards, Gardeners Guild: "Get the best tools you can for the job and avoid DIY chains because the quality is poor and you cannot get spares. Tool dealerships are not just where tradespeople go, but where people who have big gardens go for servicing and repairs. Build a relationship with the people behind the counter and you will get work through referrals."

Mark Yabsley, Pod Garden Design: "When gardening in a recession, think positively, seek new opportunities and be more creative to find work. Be open to things you may not have considered previously and diversify your skills and services. Network more, keep your head; it is easy to become spooked by a deluge of bad news, most of which does not directly affect you. Manage your budgets wisely, deliver outstanding service and finally ride the wave as things improve. And they will."

AND FINALLY

"When gardening in a recession, think positively, seek new opportunities and be more creative to find work."

Alan Shipp, National Collection of Hyacinths: "When you embark on a business project you really have no idea of where it will ultimately lead you. In my case, a whole chain of events evolved and if just one of those links had been missing, I would not be where I am today. I embarked on the initial idea of becoming a commercial grower of hyacinths and found out about the National Hyacinth Collection, which ultimately lead to me becoming the successive collection-holder. My prominence in the field brought a contact from Lithuania. Her friend was the wife of the then Lithuanian Ambassador in London. Through these contacts I obtained incredibly rare hyacinths from all over the former Soviet Union. For the last few years I have been the UK hyacinth expert on the RHS Daffodil and Tulip Committee and, in 2012, I selected and chaired the Hyacinth Panel in the RHS Award of Garden Merit hyacinth trials at Wisley. All of the above is not what I originally set out to do!"

Resources

Askham Bryan College
Tel: 01904 772 277; web: *www.askham-bryan.ac.uk*

BALI (British Association of Landscape Industries)
Tel: 024 7669 0333; email: *contact@bali.org.uk*; web:
www.bali.org.uk

British Plant Nursery Guide
Tel: 01600 716 195; web:
www.britishplantnurseryguide.co.uk

Business Gateway Scotland
Web: *www.business.scotland.gov.uk*

Business Support Wales
Web: *www.business.wales.gov.uk*

Capel Manor College
Tel: 08456 122 122; email: *enquiries@capel.ac.uk*; web:
www.capel.ac.uk

City & Guilds
Tel: 0844 543 0033; email:
learnersupport@cityandguilds.com; web:
www.cityandguilds.com

Commercial Horticultural Association (CHA)
Web: *www.cha-hort.com*

Companies House
Tel: 0303 1234 500; email: *enquiries@companies-
house.gov.uk*; web: *www.companieshouse.gov.uk*

Eden Project
Web: *www.edenproject.com*

eFig (European Federation of Interior Landscaping Industries)
Web: *www.efig.eu.com*

Enterprise Nation
Web: *www.enterprisenation.com*

English Gardening School
Tel: 020 7352 4347; web: *www.englishgardeningschool.co.uk*

Environment Agency
Web: *www.environment-agency.gov.uk*

Federation of Small Business
Tel: 0808 2020 888; email: *customerservices@fsb.org.uk*; web:
www.fsb.org.uk

FreeAgent
Tel: 0800 288 8691; email: *hello@freeagent.com*; web:
www.freeagent.com

Garden Design Journal (Society of Garden Designers
publication)
Web: *www.gardendesignjournal.com*

Garden Design School
Tel: 01380 728 788; email: *enquiries@gardendesignschool.co.uk*;
web: *www.gardendesignschool.co.uk*

Garden Media Guild
Tel: 01989 567 393; email: *admin@gardenmediaguild.co.uk*; web:
www.gardenmediaguild.co.uk

GLEE The Garden Retail Show
Web: *www.gleebirmingham.com*

GOV.UK
Web: *www.gov.uk*

Grow (Institute of Horticulture initiative)
Web: *www.growcareers.info*

HM Revenue & Customs
Web: *www.hmrc.gov.uk*

Horticultural Trades Association
Tel: 0118 930 3132; email: *info@the-hta.org.uk*; web:
www.the-hta.org.uk

Horticulture Week
Web: *www.hortweek.com*

The HTA National Plant Show
Tel: 0118 930 3132; email:
enquiries@nationalplantshow.co.uk; web:
www.nationalplantshow.co.uk

Inchbald School of Design
Tel: 020 7630 9011; email: *gardens@inchbald.co.uk*; web:
www.inchbald.co.uk

Institute of Horticulture (and *The Horticulturist*
magazine)
Tel: 01992 707025; email: *ioh@horticulture.org.uk*; web:
www.horticulture.org.uk

KLC School of Design
Tel: 020 7376 3377; email: *info@klc.co.uk*; web:
www.klc.co.uk

Landscape Juice
Web: *www.landscapejuice.com* and
www.landscapejuicenetwork.com

LANDSCAPE Show
Tel: 020 7821 8221; web: *www.landscapeshow.co.uk*

LANTRA (training)
Tel: 02476 696 996; web: *www.lantra.co.uk*

Merrist Wood College
Tel: 01483 884 000; email: *mwinfo@guildford.ac.uk*; web:
www.merristwood.ac.uk

MFL Professional Partnerships (specialist insurance broker)
Tel: 0161 236 2532; email: *info@m-f-l.co.uk*; web: *www.m-f-l.co.uk*

National Enterprise Network
Tel: 01234 831623; email: *enquiries@nationalenterprise
network.org*; web: *www.nationalenterprisenetwork.org*

National Gardens Scheme
Tel: 01483 211 535; email: *admin@ngs.org.uk*;
web: *www.ngs.org.uk*

National Trust for Scotland School of Heritage Gardening
Tel: 0844 493 2100; email: *information@nts.org.uk*; web:
www.nts.org.uk

National Trust NT Academy
Web: *www.nationaltrustjobs.org.uk*

NPTC (City & Guilds)
Tel: 02476 857 300; email: *information@cityandguilds.com*;
web: *www.nptc.org.uk*

Perhore College
Tel: 01926 318 000; email: *info@warkscol.ac.uk*; web:
www.warwickshire.ac.uk

PRIME (Prince's Initiative for Mature Enterprise)
Tel: 0845 862 2023; email: *info@prime.org.uk*; web:
www.prime.org.uk

The Prince's Trust
Tel: (head office) 0800 842 842; email:
webinfops@princes-trust.org.uk; web: *www.princes-trust.org.uk*

Professional Gardeners Guild
Web: *www.pgg.org.uk*

Professional Garden Photographers' Association
Web: *www.gpauk.org*

Royal Botanic Gardens Edinburgh
Web: *www.rbge.org.uk*

Royal Botanic Gardens Kew
Web: *www.kew.org*

Royal Horticultural Society
Web: *www.rhs.org.uk*

Social Enterprise UK
Tel: 020 3589 4950; email: *info@socialenterprise.org.uk*;
Web: *www.socialenterprise.org.uk*

Society of Garden Designers
Tel: 01989 566 695; email: *admin@sgd.org.uk*; web:
www.sgd.org.uk

Start Ups
Web: *www.startups.co.uk*

The Association of Professional Landscapers
Tel: 0118 930 3132; email: *apl@the-hta.org.uk*; web:
www.landscaper.org.uk

The Gardeners Guild
Tel: 0845 0533 106; email:
enquiries@thegardenersguild.co.uk; web:
www.thegardenersguild.co.uk

The Garden History Society
Tel: 020 7608 2409; email:
enquiries@gardenhistorysociety.org; web:
www.gardenhistorysociety.org

The Garden Show
Tel: 01243 538 456; email: *info@thegardenshowonline.com*;
web: *www.thegardenshowonline.com*

Women's Farm & Garden Association (including WRAGS)
Tel: 01285 658 339; email: *admin@wfga.org.uk*; web:
www.wfga.org.uk

Writtle College
Tel: 01245 424 200; email: *info@writtle.ac.uk*; web:
www.writtle.ac.uk